Praise for *Re*

"The Biblical teaching on forgiveness and reconciliation has been called 'a great unnatural act.' In this autobiography, however, Antoine Rutayisire explains how it has become central to his identity and Christian experience. It is a riveting testimony of courage, conviction, and biblical radicalism. It is a deeply touching and captivating story. If you read it, expect to be moved, challenged. . . and changed."

– *Lindsay Brown, former General Secretary of International Fellowship of Evangelical Student (IFES) and International Director of the Lausanne Movement*

"I've known and closely worked with Reverend Pastor Dr. Antoine Rutayisire since 1995 when we started, together with other brothers and sisters in Christ, the Rwanda Leaders Fellowship, a lay Ministry which organizes prayer breakfasts for leaders with the purpose of instilling godly values in Rwandan leadership. I have known Antoine Rutayisire as a clear voice of healing, forgiveness and reconciliation in our nation. He was recommended as a member of our National Unity and Reconciliation Commission where he played a significant role not only as a speaker but also as a model of forgiveness.

Today, Pastor Rutayisire is probably the most trusted and loved person by Rwandans from the Hutu, Tutsi and Twa communities because he has been openly speaking the truth in love to all Rwandans. As a man of God, he has been a true ambassador of reconciliation, reconciling Rwandans with God and with themselves and has been one of the greatest contributors to the genuine reconciliation that has taken place in Rwanda. I totally agree with the title of his book that reconciliation has been his lifestyle and I highly recommend it to anyone desiring to understand Rwanda's reconciliation journey and to discover that God is indeed able to do immeasurably more than all we ask or imagine, according to his power that is at work within us, believers, and to give glory to Him."

– *Ambassador Dr. Charles Murigande, former Minister of Education, Minister of Foreign Affairs, Minister of Cabinet Affairs and Rwandan Ambassador to Japan, Australia, New Zealand, and the Philippines*

"Having worked with African Evangelistic Enterprise (AEE) in Rwanda for several years, I remember Antoine as a man of prayer whose greatest priority is hearing what God has to say and obeying it; a man of determination, wisdom and forgiveness, who is not afraid to speak the truth, whatever that costs him. I strongly recommend this book — a very honest, gripping story of the challenges of life in Rwanda before, during, and after the genocide against the Tutsi. Be warned: you will be challenged by reading this book!"

– *Rhiannon Lloyd, Welsh psychiatrist, healing and reconciliation trainer, and Director of "Healing the Nations"*

"As a survivor of the genocide against the Tutsis, like many others whenever I hear the phrase 'forgiveness, unity, and reconciliation in Rwanda, I associate these words with Dr. Pastor Antoine Rutayisire. He has been a pillar of strength and instrumental in bringing a fragmented country together. Pastor Antoine has cared for many orphans of the genocide and journeyed with many of us survivors on our search for healing. Through his work of teaching biblical wisdom, God has used him as a bridge between the broken-hearted and their perpetrators. Pastor Antoine, a survivor of the genocide himself, put aside his own pain and carried the torch of reconciliation and has been a living example of forgiveness, a true Christ follower, and an instrument of the gospel, but also a true treasure for our nation Rwanda and the world. His story will shock you, challenge you, and move you to see Christ's love through unimaginable hatred."

   - *Frida Umuhoza, Survivor, speaker, and author of Frida: Chosen to Die,*
   Destined to Live

"I was born into a 'Hutu family,' and we fled Rwanda during the war that stopped the genocide against the Tutsi in 1994 and settled for a short while in Zaire (presently known as Democratic Republic of Congo (DRC)). We came back to Rwanda in 1997. I was then 13 years old, full of fear of retaliation from the Tutsis. I was ready to die and did not have any hope for the future as I could not see a place for myself in post-genocide Rwanda. The life and ministry of the man whose book you are holding in your hands not only brought healing to my life but helped give me hope, joy, and a vision for the future. He has been a mentor, a father, and a role model to me and my family, and he has given hope to thousands of people through his life and ministry of reconciliation. This book will challenge you and stretch your faith, but also encourage you to realize that it is possible, through the cross of Jesus, to live a lifestyle of reconciliation."

   - *Lambert Bariho, Director Ellel Ministries Rwanda*

"Long before I met Pastor Antoine, I knew of him by reputation as a man who lived out what he taught, thereby securing the respect of all. Through his recollections and reflections in this book, I now understand why. When we talk about reconciliation in theory, it seems comforting and suitable for a bumpersticker, but to see it in fact and in action is profoundly disturbing. Antoine's message of forgiveness and reconciliation confronts one's own pride, fears for self-preservation, and unexamined prejudices. If you take up this book, prepare for an invitation to change and grow in the costly grace of Christ."

   - *Benjamin L. Fischer, Rector of Christ the Redeemer in Nampa, Idaho,*
   and author of Being a Pastor and Dying in Islam, Rising in Christ

RECONCILIATION
IS MY LIFESTYLE

A Life's Lesson on Forgiving and
Loving Those Who Have Hated You

ALSO IN THE LIVING RECONCILIATION SERIES
FROM PEMBROKE STREET PRESS

Dying in Islam, Rising in Christ:
Encountering Jesus Beyond the Grave
Cedric Kanana with Benjamin Fischer

RECONCILIATION
IS MY LIFESTYLE

A Life's Lesson on Forgiving and
Loving Those Who Have Hated You

Antoine Rutayisire

Foreword by Pastor Rick Warren

PEMBROKE STREET PRESS

PEMBROKE STREET PRESS

Reconciliation is My Lifestyle: A Life's Lesson on Forgiving and Loving Those Who Have Hated You
Copyright © 2021 by Antoine Rutayisire
All rights reserved. First edition 2021.

Published by Pembroke St. Press, LLC, 307 S State St., Nampa, ID 83686.

ISBN 978-0-9992904-5-3 (softcover)

Printed in the United States of America

DEDICATION

To all of you who believe this truth that blessed are the peacemakers,

To all of you, the whole world over,

Who believe life is worth living only when we love each other,

To all of you who believe

Reconciliation can be a Lifestyle.

CONTENTS

FOREWORD

RECONCILIATION IS HARD AND PAINFUL. And it is human nature to avoid hard things just like water runs into the easiest channels as it flows downhill. If we can find the easiest, least painful path, we will. But the easy path is rarely the best one, and almost all of the best things in life require moments of discomfort before they can be enjoyed. We know this is true generally, but reconciliation is a special case. With many of the good things we pursue—like better health, greater knowledge, or honed skills in something—we willingly enter the situation, make the choice, and take on the challenges and troubles. We wanted to take on the difficulty because we could see the end would be adding to us. Not so when reconciliation is needed. Most often, when the choice to pursue reconciliation is ours, it is because we have been thrust into it against our will. We have been wronged. We have been wounded. We have been sinned against. The need for reconciliation means there's has been a loss, a deficit. Far from welcoming the challenge as a path of improvement, usually we doubt that we could ever return to the condition in which we were wronged.

Few people have thought as long and as deeply about this process as my friend Antoine Rutayisire. Growing up in the tense climate of post-colonial Rwanda, in which political factions moved in and out of war and uneasy peace, he felt the constant threat of loss from his earliest years. When the losses came, they hit close and hard. He has experienced deep injustice and the catastrophic effects of others' sins. And he has found himself trapped in the terrible prison of personal bitterness. He knows what it means to feel the hopelessness of bringing the best that you can muster, only to find that a system and powers beyond your control have determined to reject you no matter what. Yet in the midst of that hopeless prison, he found Jesus Christ, who has already gone to every dark dungeon and opened the door for every captive.

11

When the time came in Rwanda to search for a path of healing, Antoine had been prepared. After learning to forgive, he was placed in a position to help a nation take its first steps of forgiveness. God had shaped him for the ministry of reconciliation, and he has been walking in that path for over twenty years. This book recounts the shaping work of God in his life and then through his life. Reading it is a bit like watching a potter at his wheel, pulling and shaping the clay into a useful vessel, and then seeing that completed vessel filled and pouring out life-giving water.

America needs this message today, but especially American Christians. In a time of political and social turmoil, as we hear voices that demonize every party and group, and as we are tempted to lump people in convenient categories in order to dismiss them, we need to be reminded that such thinking comes from the enemy of all people—the Enemy of God. We are riddled with divisions of class, and we feel the faultlines of racial and ethnic differences. Antoine's story warns about the chaos the enemy strives to unleash, but it gives the unshakeable hope that the love of God and the power of the Cross are sufficient to overcome every effort to destroy. God has given the gift of peace by his Spirit, and all who have his Spirit have the power to make peace.

But Antoine's message requires honesty. The peace of reconciliation is costly. It cost Jesus at the Cross and it costs us who take up his cross and follow him. We need Antoine's message because those who have walked that hard road can call to us and reassure, "It's worth it! Keep going!" Antoine has encouraged me that just as there was joy set before Jesus to endure the cross, there is joy set before us, too. I have long followed his good work, and I commend his message.

– *Pastor Rick Warren*
Saddleback Church

12

Foreword

Reconciliation is My Lifestyle

INTRODUCTION

RWANDA. THE COUNTRY OF A THOUSAND HILLS. The country of the mountain gorillas. The country of Hotel Rwanda. The country of the genocide against the Tutsis. Today, other adjectives and qualifiers are emerging, but that is long after the story you are about to read in this book. Historians have it that the country started as a small kingdom in the ninth century, which slowly grew to become the mighty conquering Kingdom of Rwanda that the colonialists "discovered" in the heart of Africa towards the end of the nineteenth century. The colonization of Rwanda came late because it is far inland in the central part of the African Continent. The Kingdom of Rwanda, like other kingdoms, was ruled by a king surrounded by chiefs organized around three major circles of influence: the land, the army, and the pastures. Cows were the reference of wealth, and a feudal system was built on that valuable animal possession. Whoever had cows had serfs, and the more serfs you had, the more power. Those with the cows came to be known as Tutsi, and those who did not have cows were in two other groups that made up the common people, namely the Hutus and the Batwas (or Twa).

The Tutsis were mainly the cow owners and were consequently the upper class of the society. The King of Rwanda obviously came from this group because he was the ruler and owner of everything in the land, and all the people were subject to his rule. The Hutus were mainly land farmers and artisans, but whoever managed to accumulate cows through hard work, valor at war or skill in art would move into the upper class to become Tutsi. There was even a term for that movement, it was called *kwihutura* (to take off your Hutu identity). The Twa were an independent group and were despised by the two other groups because they lived nomadically in the jungle and refused the settled lifestyle of the kingdom. History has recorded, however, that some members of this group also managed to

15

emerge and integrate into the upper class of Tutsis. This was a very fluid and mobile social organization: a Tutsi who became poor went down the ladder and started mixing with the lower class, slowly integrating into the Hutu group. A Hutu who managed to climb the ladder through accumulation of cows and influence became Tutsi. Some Twa managed to join the elite class through favor from the King. That is the society the colonialists found when they arrived in the late 19th century.

At the Berlin Conference of 1884-1885, when representatives of the European colonial powers met in Berlin to divide Africa between them, Rwanda fell on the German plate and became a German colony for a few years (1896-1919). When Germany lost World War I, it also lost all its colonies, and Rwanda became a Belgian protectorate under the Society of Nations in 1919. Belgium ruled Rwanda as a colony and organized it on social terms that confused the social classes of Hutus, Tutsis, and Twas into ethnic groups. They registered all the adults, male and female, and distributed identity cards that were ethnically marked Hutu, Tutsi or Twa; thus, a social system that used to be fluid and mobile became rigid and fixed. They favored the Tutsi chiefs for education and all positions of power, which created resentments in the general population.

In the 1950s, many African countries started claiming and gaining independence from their colonial masters, and the King of Rwanda made the same claim. The Belgian administration eliminated him in very obscure circumstances, and then turned the population against each other, using the ethnic groups they had created. Ethnic based political parties mushroomed everywhere, and despite being a small country we had around nineteen political parties. Trying to retain influence, the colonial powers supported the birth of political parties but favored one political party called MDR-Parmehutu over any other. Within this political turmoil, the long-building resentments from the colonial era sparked off mass killings against the Tutsis that sent many people into exile between 1959-1963. Eventually, Rwanda became a republic in the hands of Hutu presidents, while the Tutsis who left the country were refused peaceful return and remained in refugee settlements in neighboring countries namely Uganda, Burundi, Tanzania, Congo, and even Kenya. The Tutsis who stayed in the country were subjugated to injustices, oppression, and sporadic mass killings as in 1966, 1973, and eventually the genocide of 1990-1994.

The younger generation of Tutsis who grew in the refugee settlements grouped themselves into a political front—the Rwanda Patriotic Front (RPF)—with a military wing—the Rwanda Patriotic Army (RPA). On October 1, 1990, the RPA began an attack on the country from Uganda. The offensive came at a time when the country was facing many other challenges, politically and economically. From the perspective of the Tutsis in exile and those under oppression inside the country, the offensive was considered as a liberation war to restore a balance of power, but it was exploited by the Hutu regime to ignite anger and hatred against the Tutsis as an ethnicity. This propaganda led to the 1990-1994 genocide against the Tutsis that took more than 1 million lives in just a hundred days between April and July 1994. This is a simplistic and simplified presentation of a rather complex reality, but this survey gives a necessary background to understand the story you are about to read.

This book has been baking in the oven of my heart for over 25 years. It is a mixture of meditation, reflection, and study. Coming out of the genocide against the Tutsi in 1994, I was in total confusion. How shall we live? How shall we relate to each other in the aftermath of such a tragedy? How shall I go out and preach about a loving God after seeing what I had seen? What message could we bring to the world? For my personal sanity, I needed to process what I had lived through, and as I sorted through it all, I learned lessons that I wanted to share with other people. This book is the end product of a journey of many years with many stops and delays.

I first published *Faith Under Fire: Testimonies of Christian Bravery* in 1996, which was a collection of testimonies—both good and bad—of how Christians behaved during the genocide. Had God left and failed us? Where was our faith? How could such a thing happen in a country where 90% of the population claimed to be Christians? How could Christians betray and kill other Christians? So many questions! Processing all the stories I had collected brought a sense of perspective to my life. My final conclusion was that God was with us, weeping with us inside the genocide, rescuing us and providing for us in many ways despite what we were seeing around us. Writing those stories did a lot of good for my inner life, but I felt there was still much inside I had not explored. In an attempt to exorcise the demons of woundedness, anger, and hatred, I decided to write my personal story of the griefs and pains that tore apart my country.

When I re-entered the writing process, I found it did me great good to go into the dark corners of my past and then glean as many lessons as I could from my experience. I started writing and kept going until I found I had written pages and pages, as if to get rid of all those horrible mementos that were bottled inside my soul. I have found that writing this book has helped me in many ways. It did me a great deal of good to explore the recesses of my heart, and I was astonished to find many wounds of my past still hidden, yet open, inside some of its corners. I have to confess I wept while working through some of the chapters, but this gave me great internal release. Digging deep into my past has helped me to understand myself better by unveiling the hidden roots of many of my present behaviors. So thank you, dear reader, for reading my story; it humbles me. Perhaps you can share this healing experience with me as you reflect on your own life.

I wish that all who lived through the horrors of Rwandan history and other similar tragedies in human history the world over, even all the Mr. and Ms. Nobodies, would dare to take time for this kind of pilgrimage into their past. I am sure this would help them heal and build a better future, free from the hidden oppression of their individual past. Such personal healing is the first step toward reconciliation and healing as a nation.

Working on *Faith under Fire* in 1995 did much good to my soul, helping me see clearly where our country was coming from and where it should be heading. It rebuilt my confidence in our humanity at a time when the genocide had negatively tainted our national image in the eyes of the whole world. My prayer at the end of the book was to see the Lord healing our nation and leading us onto the path of reconciliation. It is now 27 years after the tragic events of the genocide against the Tutsi and the war that was waged to stop it. Everybody has now heard great stories of healing, unbelievable tales of forgiveness, amazing accounts of repentance and confession, and magnificent reports of reconciliation. I am glad I was alive to see it and even be among the agents of that change, giving my small contribution here and there. This book, *Reconciliation is My Lifestyle*, is a personal story of healing and reconciliation, woven with gems of wisdom gleaned from different experiences as a preacher of reconciliation and as a Commissioner on the National Unity and Reconciliation Commission.

This is a book of hope, written to tell you that it is possible to be thrown into the furnace of hatred and death and come out shining bright, "without the smell of smoke." I hope this book will help many to see that it is possible to go through the fire and come out rather purified, tempered, and unbound. I hope reading this book will encourage many who are thrown into a life furnace—a divorce, a betrayal, a failure—to take that road of healing and find freedom through the fire. Let every reader of this book say, *Reconciliation is My Lifestyle.*

– Antoine Rutayisire, 2020.

MAP OF RWANDA

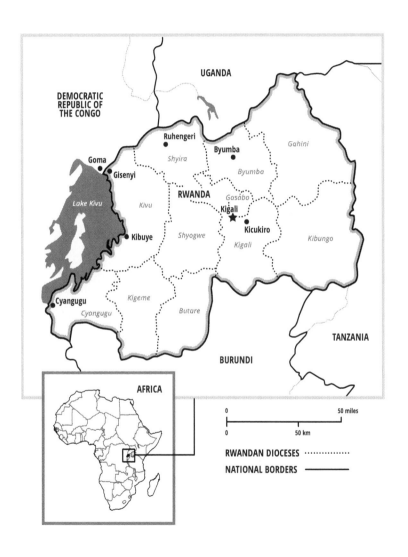

Chapter One

THE BITTER SEEDS
OF HATRED

"Like a mustard seed which a man took and planted...."
Matthew 13:31

ON THE SHORE of the beautiful valley lake of Muhazi, the village of Ntete sits on a projecting flat. The lake hugs it in a lovely embrace, and were it not for the one kilometer of dry land joining it to the next village, the village would be an island. This village, where I was born and grew up, has always boasted of being the pilot project for model rural living established by King Mutara Rudahigwa in 1955. The dirt road dug during that period coils around the village like a snake biting its own tail. Each family had a large plot of land divided into smaller plots designated for different crops: a plot for coffee, a plot for fruit trees (this was a novelty), a plot for cassava, a plot for potatoes, a plot for banana trees, a plot for vegetables, and a pasture for cattle. The houses were built with adobe bricks and roofed with corrugated iron sheets. This house style, too, was new and was the pride of our village. In all the other villages around us — stretching as far as eyes could see — people were still living in grass thatched huts while I was growing up.

My family had one of these modern houses, but we still lived and slept in our grass thatched hut because the iron corrugated roof made the house hot — spoiling milk and melting butter during the day and disturbing sleep at night because of its cracking noises. In fact, not many families slept or lived in their modern houses, although they kept them clean and equipped for when officials visited. The villagers had been ordered to build the houses; the king supplied the brick-making machines, the iron sheets, and timber; and all the houses were built following the same model. Therefore, these structures were nicknamed *Inzu za Rudahigwa*, "the houses of King Rudahigwa" — as if he was the one living in them!

On the whole, life was good and contented in this village where I grew up. People who spoke strange languages often came to visit our village (sometimes just to buy different fruits). We always ran to see the white visitors in the cars and enjoyed imitating them, mimicking the "twang" sounds through the nose and rolling our tongues.

I don't know which day of the week or even which month I was born. Only the year is sure, 1958. When I was baptized as a child, the priest wrote that I was born on May 29, 1958, but based on what my mother tells me, my best guess is that I was born some time late July or early August. I was always told I was born when they had finished harvesting sorghum, and you never harvest sorghum in May. I use the 29th of May on all my papers, and sometimes I even celebrate my birthday on that date; my wife surprises me with gifts and my children sing "happy birthday to you, dad," but deep inside I know the date does not mean much. One thing is sure, I was born some time and it is good to celebrate. I was the second child and the second son born to my family.

My mother tells me I was a very fragile child when I was born, and they feared I would not survive long. From the very first day of my birth until I was one and a half years old, I cried most of the time, and they could not figure out why. Medical services in the area were not very developed yet, and you had to walk a long distance to get to the nearest dispensary. All our children were born *mu gikari*, in the backyard of our compound, just behind the house. That was the private area of every compound — where adult people took their bath under the cover of night, and where they sat when the diviner would cast lots to tell the future. Only intimate friends and members of the family were allowed to use the back gate into the *gikari*. On the eighth day, the day of the naming ceremony, I was still very sick and weak. They were not sure I was going to live even another week. Out of desperation and maybe out of some hope, my father gave me the name Rutayisire, which means "if death does not take him." I don't know what he meant with that unfinished sentence as a name, but I prefer to think he meant something positive like, "If death does not take him, he will grow up to be a man." After all, that is the cherished wish every Rwandan father has for his newborn son. That is why many boys are given names of bravery and courage. My elder brother was called Rutembesa, "the one who makes enemies fall in battle," and my younger brother was named Rudasingwa, "the unbeatable in battle," and I was named Rutayisire, "if death does not take him...."

It is possible that Dad was afraid to give me a strong male name out of fear of disappointment in case I died in early childhood. But I prefer to believe he gave me that unfinished sentence for a name as a blank sheet to fill with all the good wishes he had for my life. "If death does not take him, he will grow up to be...." How prophetic! I have met death face to face many times but am still alive, having narrowly survived. On other occasions I guess Dad meant that name as a prayer. For those who do not know Rwandan culture well, let me add that we are very particular about naming our children. For example, a child is not given the name of his or her parents, or a family last name — every child is given his or her own name. Today we are seeing the encroachment of foreign practices such as naming children after their parents; sometimes one might now hear the new peculiarity of a girl with a male name! But that is modernity, and it brings its own oddities.

I remember my early childhood well. Our home was peaceful, and life was especially pleasant. My father was a businessman and a farmer; neither of my parents had been to school but both knew how to read. He had a small shop, two fishing boats on Lake Muhazi, and a good plot of land where they produced lots of crops and grazed some cattle. Dad was a very jovial man, and I don't remember ever hearing him quarrel with Mum. He was always gentle with us, only scolding us on exceptional occasions when we stepped beyond the boundaries of what we knew he expected from us. Those infrequent times he spanked us are burned into memory, due to his unique method. He would first ask you to go out and bring a medium branch, then you were asked to spell out the cause of your punishment before getting the right amount of spanking. You could easily be forgiven if you were fast enough to ask for clemency immediately after recognizing your offense. This exercise was more humiliating than a whipping, and I remember at times not asking for forgiveness. I got my share of spankings as I always enjoyed playing the trickster of the family. I vividly remember two occasions when my pleas went unheard: one time when I had colored Dad's puppy dog with white chalk and cow dung to make it black and white like a zebra and another time when I was caught trying to convince my younger sister to play "husband and wife."

Dad was a very caring father, and he wanted us to always look clean, neat, and happy. He often bought new clothes for us and always brought us sweets when he came back from his frequent "import" trips. He would travel to Uganda by bicycle to purchase the goods he sold in his village shop. Although I do not actually know how long those trips took him, I always had the impression it was a long time because of my impatient waiting for the sweets to come. The distance from our place to the border with Uganda is only 100 km, but I suspect the roads were poor then, and it must have been a slow journey by bicycle.

When Dad was away, our mother always entertained us with stories, riddles, and songs. Storytelling was part of our evenings when all the house chores were finished. Only one family in the whole village had a radio, and at times we could hear its loud music blaring in the silence of the evenings, but we could not go there to listen at night. I always dreamed of the day when Dad would get rich enough to buy a radio, but I loved our stories nonetheless. There were many reasons for this. Mother told good stories, and I always outwitted my elder brother and cousins at oratorical games she led us in playing. My brother was slow with his tongue, and he tended to stammer under pressure. He actually grew up to be a peaceful and quiet person, always shying away from public exposure. But I took every pleasure and opportunity to show off my linguistic and rhetorical capabilities.

I cannot remember how it all began, but all of a sudden, things started going wrong all around our village. We had many visitors who would come stealthily into our home by night and leave very early before dawn. They spoke in murmurs and hushed tones. They often came when we had gone to bed and always stayed in the corrugated iron roofed house; I rarely managed to even catch a word of what they were saying. But I once overheard they were fleeing from their villages on the other side of the lake, going to Uganda.

In the far distance, we could at times see high flames blanching the night and coloring the horizon red, and my brother told me those were houses being set on fire. The fires, the night movements, the worried faces of my parents, and the people who often traveled by our place — all these things told my young inquisitive mind that something had definitely gone wrong despite the adults' attempts to keep us unaware so that we would not worry.

The singing had gone out of my mother; the stories and the riddles were no longer there. Evenings felt tense. We ate early, then went to bed in silence. Daytime was now characterized by a great deal of movement. Some people were still trekking with their families, but we could not figure out exactly what was going on. We knew that people were fleeing, but that did not mean much to us. Then, for the first time I saw helicopters flying over our village. They would drop pieces of paper all over the place; although we collected them, we did not know how to read and they meant nothing to us. We were always told to be careful not to be seen burning or tearing these papers. "The Mzungu (white people) may find out and you will be in trouble," we were always warned. We finally decided it was safer not to touch the papers, and whenever they were thrown near us, we simply ran away and hid as if from a plague.

Stories were spreading that the helicopters had burnt houses in some villages and that they had even cut some people's necks with those gigantic "machetes" (the helicopter blades) that were always swinging menacingly while in motion. We feared the helicopters, and every time we heard their drone from over the hill, we ran for safety and took care to always hide our necks. Their visits were dreadful, and I remember I started getting nightmares where I was pursued by a fast helicopter — but I always outran it and survived its chase. I was Rutayisire, "if death does not take him," even in my nightmares!

Things went from bad to worse when soldiers in jeeps that we called *Kavure* (or trough, because they were not covered on top) started coming into the village. These Congolese soldiers were called *Kamina* (later I learned this was the name of the training camp where they came from in Congo), and they were the terror of women and children. We were told to keep our distance from them. It was rumored that they raped women and ate children. Every time we heard their jeeps on the road, the whole village would hide in the bushes, women running as fast as they could so as not to be seen. Life was becoming a nightmare even for us children. We were told the big sticks (rifles) the soldiers carried on their shoulders could spit fire and kill. More reason not to even think of getting nearer to these terrible people. The helicopters, the jeeps, and the helmeted soldiers just meant death and terror to us, although we had never seen anybody killed. But stories were repeatedly told of villages that had been burnt, of people who had been cruelly killed. Fear filled our hearts. I did not like the coming of night when we had to go to bed early, switch off the kerosene lamp, and scatter the fire in the hearth so as not to attract the attention of the soldiers. I hated the hushed conversations and the nights when we were beaten into silence so we would not draw attention. The songs were gone, the stories were dead. Fear and silence had raided our nights.

Soon the problems became more local and invasive. One of our neighbors' thatched house was burnt to ashes and he was beaten. We watched nearby, and when the mob left, one of the vandals swung his club in our direction and shouted, "Tomorrow, it is you!" The threat did not mean much to our young minds, but the following day around noon when we brought home the calves from pasture, we found Mum and Dad in total silence. I immediately felt that something had gone amiss, but still we were not too anxious. Later, food was served for lunch, and as soon as we started eating a whistle was blown at the entrance of our compound. Then came heavy thumping and thunderous shouting, and a mob made up of people from our neighborhood and from other parts of the village broke into the compound like a swarm of bees. Dad stood up and silently walked out to meet them. I cannot remember what they told him or how he answered; the next minute he was on the ground screaming, groaning. The mob of our neighbors swarmed on top of him, beating him with their sticks and clubs. Some of them came inside the house. One took the food we were eating and threw it outside. He took the tin mugs of milk Mum had just poured for us and spilled them all on the ground. We nestled onto our mother's side and stayed with her.

"Get out of our way, you bitch, and take out your puppies with you," one of the vandals said, brandishing his big club in her face. We rushed out to give way to those who were plundering our valuables. We sat in a corner of the compound, shivering with fear, nestled behind our weeping mother. Dad lay there, motionless in a pool of blood while the mob went on with their ghastly business. They took things out of the house, choosing what to take and breaking to pieces what they did not want. Before long, our home looked like a ruin, and all our possessions were either taken or broken.

All of a sudden, as if from a new inspiration, one of the ruffians rushed toward us brandishing his nail-spiked club over our heads, gnarling like an angry dog, a devilish look in his eyes. I don't know if he was just scaring us, but I still believe he really meant to knock our brains out. But one of his cohorts came from behind him and caught his arm in the air before he could bring his lethal weapon down.

"Don't!" he shouted to him, "the blood of women and innocent children brings back luck." He stopped and moved away, dragging his feet, pulled away by his friend.

When the looting was over, they left the compound, carrying their booty, singing their macabre song "Turatsinze ga ye, turatsinze" — "we have won, we have won." When I grew up I came to learn that this was the anthem of the MDR-Parmehutu Party, but for me it was to remain the song of thugs and murderers.

Mum was paralyzed by fear, and we did not know what would come next. Were they coming back? It was as if time had stopped. Eventually Mum moved to where Dad lay in a small drying pool of blood and turned him to see if he was still alive. They had not used their machetes but had just beaten him with their clubs. One had given him a heavy blow on the head with his hammer. Blood stopped flowing from his wounds, but his whole body was covered with wounds and welts, and his face was swollen. Fortunately, he was still breathing. Mum went inside and got some water from the pot the mob had not broken, and she started cleaning his wounds. Eventually, Dad opened his eyes, and Mum helped him inside the house. Since I was only a child, I did not perceive time accurately; however, I remember Dad was in bed for a long time and could not move without help.

Once a wealthy family, we had become poor, and our lives had to be rebuilt as my father slowly recovered. Peace finally returned; the helicopters were no longer flying over us, and the jeeps and soldiers were nowhere to be seen. It does not take long for children to recover from shock; we were playing again and mother resumed telling her stories and singing us the lullabies while Dad returned to business as usual, including his trips to

Uganda. It seemed like normal life again with all its joys and laughter (even the sweets). In spite of this, deep inside, some bad seeds had been sown in my heart. I always wondered why our neighbors had done that to us. Why did they beat my father? Why did they destroy and take our possessions? Why did that man want to kill us with his nail-spiked club? Mixed feelings stirred in my heart, a jumble of fear and hatred for those people.

I even started thinking that the day I grew up and became strong enough, I would avenge my father as heroes did in some of the stories Mum told us at night. The image of the neighbor with the nail-spiked club stayed with me, seared deep in my memory. After all, these were neighbors, people we had to see again and again, living next to each other in the same community. Every time I met him, even years later when I had grown up, I always saw him through that fateful day, envisioning that devilish snarling grin on his face and his arm lifted high over our heads with his spiked club. And I always told myself "one day when I grow up, I will kill this man or one of his children." All those evil visions would parade in front of me every time I remembered that day – and it was often. In my daydreams, I would see the men throwing our food out and pouring our milk on the ground, I would see the one who took my new shorts and carried them away wearing them on his head like a hat. And the spiked club and the ferocious dog snarl. Those images never left me; my mind was seared with them. These were the dreadful memories, sad memories that were to haunt my sleep, turning my dreams into nightmares. These were tormenting souvenirs that I would always remember every time something went wrong in my life.

I am now grown up and have had time to process all those sad events. I have succeeded in exorcising my demons. I no longer feel the anger welling inside me when I remember my past. I have learned to accept the reality that the balance of revenge will never be even. We will never get even with our tormentors, and I no longer nurse the desire for vengeance. Since then, I have gone through worse situations and have learned to cope with any unpleasant circumstance. I am now confident I can keep my sanity under any condition as long as I keep control over my mind and my emotions. I know how to forgive. I know how to love, even the unloving, even the unlovable, even the enemy. Reconciliation has become my lifestyle.

But I am now worried about our younger generation. Many have seen their parents massacred. Some have even seen their fathers killing their mothers. Almost all our young adults in their late 20's and 30's have seen or heard somebody being killed. Some have even been encouraged to take part in killing. And I wonder, Will they all heal from those memories? How shall we exorcise those demons to create a future generation not haunted by the evil they have witnessed? Lord, inspire us to bring up a generation of healthy individuals and communities, delivered from the nightmares of our past, a generation dreaming constructive dreams, not churning thoughts of evil and revenge.

Chapter Two

STOLEN CHILDHOOD, STOLEN LAUGHTER

"A man's spirit sustains him in sickness,
But a crushed spirit who can bear"
Prov. 18:14

CHILDREN OFTEN HAVE NO NOTION of minutes passing, less so of hours and years. Talking to my mother, I was astonished to find out that the impressions and moments I have put together in the previous chapter span a period of three years (1960-1963), and although the facts and details are accurate, it has been impossible to piece these stories together on a precise time line. While sorting through my past, I was amazed to see how selective my memory has been — bad memories surviving, arranging themselves prominently amidst a confused maze of sensations. Survival mechanisms preprogram our minds to work against us, storing more memories of the evil done against us and hardly any of the good.

After his recovery from the attack, Dad rebuilt his business with more determination, and it seems he did even better than before, despite his frequent health problems resulting from the beatings. During that time a baby boy was added to our family. Life rolled back to normal, but only for a short while. The mobs with clubs and sticks reappeared, but this time doing night rounds. Rumor had it that a group called *Inyenzi* — who were Tutsis — had attacked the country from the North in Umutara, and everybody had been asked to watch out for any of them who might be infiltrating. People started coming to our place by night again; the murmurings and hushed voices were back. My elder brother had started school, and he always came back with sad stories he heard from his classmates. He told me about the *Inyenzi*, and that Tutsis in Rwanda were being killed for being Tutsis. He also talked about how many Tutsis were fleeing. But I was too young to grasp the full meaning of what was going on.

Who were those Tutsis being killed? Who were those Tutsi *Inyenzi* who had attacked the country? And why should that affect our life? What had we done? I knew the stories and the facts, but they did not mean much to me. My brother did not know any more than I did, though he too was learning to communicate in hushed murmurs.

One night, Dad left with a group of the whispering men who had come to our home by night. I assumed he had gone on one of his lengthy "import" trips and that he would come back. I waited, often standing on the road looking in the direction he used to come from, expecting to see him from the distance and dash to greet him as we always did. But he did not come. Every night, I saw Mum weeping or heard her sobbing in bed, and she grew less and less inclined to tell stories. Lullabies for our younger brother (who was just a small baby) were rarer and very sorrowful when they came. A mist of gloom had descended upon our family, and we did not know why. As time went by, Mum became more unpredictable. She would be joyful some days, telling us stories and singing us the happy old songs, and then the following day she would be moody and ill-tempered. And in my childish innocence and ignorance, I blamed the gloom and other problems on Dad, who was taking too long to come back home.

It was obvious that one of those problems was financial; some of the things we used to enjoy seemed to have left with father. The tougher that life became, the greater my expectations grew to see Dad coming back home. I knew he had the answer . . . but for some reason he was not coming back. As time passed, Mum stopped crying, but she was no longer the same. She started waking us up very early, often pushing us out of bed with harsh words, telling us it was high time we behaved and acted like real men. This did not mean much to us, but life had definitely changed.

We started getting up before daybreak, and each boy was assigned duties around the house. My brother was in full charge of everything having

33

to do with the cows — taking them to the pastures, watering them, and cutting grass for their litter in the compound. My job was fetching water and firewood, cleaning the compound, fetching grass for the calves, and helping milk the cows. My elder brother was 8 and I was 6! My younger sister was only 3 by then, and my younger brother was still a baby. Mum took to the fields with frenzy and started producing a lot more of everything and selling surplus in the market.

Life was more or less comfortable again but at the same time hard. There was no time to play or linger. Life was just work and more work as everybody was struggling to finish his share of the daily tasks. The songs and stories were still there in the evenings, but we often came home too tired, sleeping in the middle of the stories and losing interest in the riddles. We went to bed very early in order to wake up very early. Time was like a taskmaster hanging over our heads; everyone had to be focused and disciplined in order to survive. Think fast, act fast, and do everything well. Rest and leisure were no longer part of our routine, except when work was over at night. Mum was still gentle to us, but we could tell she was under emotional stress, tired, and lonely. As I look back, I guess life was becoming too hard to handle, as she was struggling to fill the roles of two parents.

My parents had settled in the model village far from their families, so when my mum was left alone with us at the age of 25, she was without any family around to help her. She didn't know how to bring up four children, especially young boys that she wanted to see grow into real men. Her dismay often showed when she lost her temper. She would beat us one instant and come pampering us with hugs and explanations the next.

"You should understand I do all this for your good. I really want you to grow up into men and not sissies. Nobody should ever say 'you are a woman's boys.' When you grow up you will understand," she often told us, apologetically.

And she did treat us like men. We were fed like men — never, for instance, given churned milk because men do not drink that kind of milk in our culture. For those who do not know, African churned milk is the milk from which they have removed butter. They will collect milk from different cows into a container, let it ferment for two or three days until it solidifies into yoghurt, then put it in a large gourd and shake it for one or two hours, separating the butter that is removed. The remaining milk is never given to men; it is for children and women. Although I preferred the skimmed milk, I had to be a man. It did not take long for us to feel we were "men" and not children. Boys in bodies, yes, but men in mind. Thinking responsibly, acting responsibly, hiding our emotions and tears — acting like men. The spontaneity of childhood was dead in us.

Today, six decades later, I have not yet recovered from that training. I have lost hope for that. I always feel an uneasy guilt when I spend time just talking or chatting, except when the conversation has to do with something serious. Small talk, socializing, and trivial conversation quickly bore me. I appreciate a joke once in a while and some laughter, but otherwise things must seem significant to concern me, becoming interesting only when they can add some meaning to life. Taking vacations is still a burden. I always find myself drifting back into some kind of work. Staying in bed when I am not asleep makes me tired and burdened, and visiting places for a long time is more of a punishment than a pleasure. I often take a book with me when I go out on group tours and turn to reading when there is nothing that seems worth watching. Many friends have often been disappointed with me and have even been offended by my behavior, but I guess it will take a long time to grow back what was uprooted from my character when my childhood was wrenched away so early.

My wife has finally given up on me when it comes to window shopping. What else would you expect from a man who was trained to be a man when he was just a child! As I write this, my heart goes out to the many children who are today worse off than I was. At least I had a mother to go to; today many of our children are heading families because they have lost their parents: either to the genocide, the war, or to diseases. I weep for you, children, who have to wake up earlier and go to bed later than others. I cry with you, children, who have lost the blessedness of innocence, you who no longer can afford the luxury of playing with the butterflies and watching the ants hatch from their eggs; you who have been forced to be prematurely responsible. I find myself echoing Alan Paton's grief for his South Africa: "Cry, my beloved country," and help us, world, to weep for those babies who have been robbed of their breast milk and whose eyes have lost the soft looks of innocence only to stare into the future with the blank gaze of premature adulthood!

In September 1965, Mum took me to school on the opening day. Many parents had brought their children to register, and the queue was quite long by the time we reached the school. I was well dressed in my new khaki uniform and was proud to see that I was better off than some of the children who did not have shorts and had come only in shirts. Remember, this was Rwanda, 1965! Small things carried great weight.

At the registration table a teacher was asking each child's name and a list of questions: Who are your parents? Are they dead or alive? These and other identifying details would be recorded in his notebook. Then my turn eventually came. "Name of child?" came the question. "Antoni Rutayisire," went back mum's answer. "Date of birth?" "1958." "Name of father?" "Karasira Petero Claver," came back the answer. "Alive?" went the question. Mum hesitated. She looked at me and then said hesitantly, in almost a whispered, "No, dead." All of a sudden, it was as if the sky had fallen on my shoulders. "Dead." The word hung in the air. My father is "dead." "No! My father is not dead, he has gone to Uganda to bring goods, and he is coming back someday soon." My mind was swirling in a whirl-wind of thoughts while I was standing there silent, tears already welling in my eyes. For such a long time I had never imagined that Dad was dead. Mum had never told us. And I was expecting him to come back any day with all the answers to our problems. And now she had said it, publicly: "dead." My dad was dead!.

Karasira Petero Claver: alive? No, dead. I kept my brave countenance. Tears were blurring my sight, but I remembered that I was a man, and men do not show their tears. We have a proverb: "the tears of a man flow into his stomach," not from his eyes. But that day, all of a sudden, I was no longer a man. My tears were too big to flow into my stomach, and I started sobbing with no explanation, to the great dismay of my mother. We hurried away from school, and I went home not just weeping but loudly wailing the whole way, like a child that has been severely beaten.

Mum kept reminding me that I was a man and that men do not cry in public and that people would laugh at me. Nothing could contain my tears. It was as if all of a sudden all the tears that I had dammed inside had suddenly found an outlet. Mum was so embarrassed by my behavior that we finally took a short cut through the pastures, away from the main road.

I wept all the way home, no matter how she tried to comfort me.

"Name of Father?" "Karasira Petero Claver." "Alive?" "No, dead." These words stayed with me, and the shock of the discovery soon metamorphosed into a heavy, vague feeling of anger mixed with the bitter disappointment of shattered hopes. Karasira Petero Claver. My dad. Dead. He is dead. He will not come back. We will never see him again. Dead with the answers; gone with the solutions to our problems. Dead, my father is dead. My mind became like a broken tape recorder, repeating the same words over and over again.

A cloak of gloom descended upon my soul, and I lost my manhood. I was still acting responsible, waking up early and doing my chores, but I was weeping inside all the time. Sometimes the tears would betray me and brim over on the outside. For no reason, I would just stand there in the dark of the night and weep. I often ran from school to do my house chores, weeping along the way and wiping my tears so people would think it was sweat. Mum started beating me for that, reminding me I was growing into a disappointment, but nothing could dry my tears. These tears stayed with me when I was growing up, sometimes returning even when I had reached the age when you do not cry. Even today, I cry when I pray for orphans; I cry when I pray for widows; my tears flow when I am asked to pray for evil in the world.

Until recently, I had always believed that I was totally healed and healthy in my inner man; that is, until I started writing this chapter. I have to confess that writing some of these paragraphs has been very painful. I was sitting in the Crowne Lounge of KLM in Amsterdam when I began this chapter, but I had to delay my writing because tears kept flooding and blurring my sight; I had to blow my nose continuously as if all of a sudden I had flu. It was as if I was back in time and the pain returned with the same heaviness. This pilgrimage into my childhood has brought many past details to my awareness that I had never taken time to fully process before. Sitting with these reflections in the light of God's story for my life has brought a clarity of meaning and acceptance, mixed with an acute sense of responsibility and commitment toward others who have suffered and are suffering the same fate, particularly when they are young.

I eventually started asking why and how my father had died. Mum never told us, but later on I found out from other boys whose fathers had suffered the same fate. In the last week of December 1963, Tutsi who had left the country and were living in refugee settlements in Uganda and Burundi grouped themselves into an army and attacked the country. I don't know why they were called *Inyenzi* (cockroaches). In retaliation, the Hutu government inside the country gave orders to round up all the influential Tutsi men who had not left the country — including businessmen and civil servants. They were taken to prisons, and later on they were shot. Some of the victims were taken to the Rusumo Falls and thrown into the Akagera River alive. None of the families were given the right to bury their dead, but the bodies were left in open fields, carcasses for dogs and birds of prey.

It was during that time my father was caught and murdered. Our district mayor (at that time the mayors were called *bourgmestres* and the districts were called "Communes") was a man called Gashugi, and he has entered history as one of the most cruel mayors throughout the country in those days. He killed so many people that all of his victims' children grew up hating him and his children. I will speak more of him and his children later.

People often claim that time heals all wounds and that anger and bitterness will die off with the years. But it does not work that way. Anger and hatred are like mud thrown into clean water. The water may eventually clear and recover its color, but even the slightest motion stirring up the bottom will quickly show that the mud is still down there, influencing and clouding its composition. When kept inside, anger does not disappear with time; it turns into bitterness and subtly distorts your whole outlook on life and your perception of other people.

The older I grew the more my anger and hatred grew with me; each life problem brought me back to the past, feeding the bitter root of my hate with new material. Why would these people kill my father? They must be bad, would come the conclusion. And every time I saw them, I just hated them. And their children were growing with us. I always told myself that "These, too, are as bad as their fathers, and one day for sure they will try to kill us." I have never been violent in my life, but I often dreamed of an opportunity when I would be able to do something big, something that could hurt these people and make them weep as many tears of sorrow as I often did.

Chapter Three

ROOTED IN HATRED

"Make sure there is no root among you that produces such bitter poison"
Deuteronomy 29:18

GOING TO SCHOOL was one of the pleasures of my life, but it also added to my problems. My chores at home were still the same, but I had to be at school by 8 o'clock each morning. Children who were tardy were always punished, most of the time by having to kneel outside in front of their classroom so that everybody who saw would know you were one of the lazy sluggards who drag their feet to school. It was a great shame. If it became a chronic problem, you were sent home to bring your father for a parent-teacher consultation. I was never late to the point of being punished, but that meant I had to wake up earlier than usual, do many chores quickly, and rush to school — six kilometers from home. I don't remember ever walking to or from school; I was always running, and fast. There was no time for camaraderie, playing, or just lingering on the way; every minute was precious.

I was among the bright ones in class, and after the first term in Primary One, our teacher decided to have me try two years at once. I was in grade one in the morning and did grade two in the afternoon, with the same teacher teaching both classes. Both the opportunity and the challenge gave me a sense of pride and achievement, as very few children had ever been permitted to make this attempt. Notwithstanding the extra pressure on my life because of the assigned chores at home, at the end of the second term I was top student in Primary One and 5th in Primary Two. At the end of that year I was promoted into grade three, having done two years in one. I attribute this success to my mum's zeal, who had taught me to read and count between our different chores.

My sister soon joined me at the same school, and she too proved to be very bright. Envy is a besetting sin in traditional villages, and being top of the class often attracted jealousy and hatred from some of the other village children. But it was always a secret pleasure to see we were ahead of them; it was like a subtle revenge on the children of those Hutus who had killed our father. It comforted my fragile sense of self, and I suspect it made them feel inferior because they often wrote nasty graffiti against us on the leaves of sisals and banana trees bordering our way to school. My sister has never forgotten one graffiti on a sisal leaf that called her a "Tutsi snake of a girl," plus an obscene insult that she spent days weeping over and still talks about. But they never dared touch her. The other pupils respected me because of the good standing I had in the school. The practice at that time was to publicly announce the class rankings for the term in the presence of all the children and their parents; the top three of every class always got a prize. For the five years I spent in that school, I was able to hold my head high three times a year as top of my class.

At home, life followed the same exhausting cycle — waking up early, doing the chores, running to school, coming back to do the evening chores. Day in and day out, it was the same life. But as my sister grew up, my work burden became lighter as she took over the compound cleaning and cooking. When time came for the national exams for secondary school, I was again quite proud of my performance: out of our school only I and one other student passed the national exam. But I decided not to go to the school the Ministry of Education had chosen for me; instead, I chose a Roman Catholic Junior Seminary. Every time I look back, I see the hand of God in this decision.

Let me explain my choice. Our village did not have a church building, and people had to walk 16 kilometers (about 10 miles) to get to the parish, the only church in our region. It was a very tiring walk, but most did not make the journey every Sunday. All the children enjoyed Christmas and

Easter when we would make the long trip to church at Kiziguro Catholic Parish. We had to leave home before dawn to be there on time for the service around 9 a.m. I was 8 years old the first time I went to church, making the ten-mile trek from my home! The church building left me in awe; I had never imagined that such a big building could exist. Even today, I am still impressed by the crushing immensity of those old brick structures. "Wow, if God has such a big house, he must be quite rich and very big," I told myself! "When I die I must go to heaven and see Him face to face. If He has such a big house here on earth, then up there in heaven where He lives it must be something else," I kept musing. Once inside the church building, my eyes were captured by a big white and blue statue of the Virgin Mary. Everybody who passed it seemed filled with respect; many crossed themselves, others knelt at its feet with reverence, and others went nearer and kissed the statue's feet. I was deeply impressed, and all the time we spent in the church, my eyes were glued on the beauty of that statue. Deep inside I kept telling myself, "If this woman really lives in heaven, then I must go there! I must see her for real." We sat in the church building, reciting our prayers and waiting for the mass to start.

My dreams of heaven were disrupted by a bell ringing from one corner of the church, and the whole congregation stood up. The procession was coming. Children in white robes were jingling small bells in front of the priest, who was dressed in very impressive colorful robes, majestically dangling a bright censer that spread a sweet-smelling smoke throughout the church. A choir I had not even noticed until then started singing from a high balcony on the northern side of the building. "Gloooo,ooo,oooria, in excelsis Deo," raised the soft voices. It was as if the sound were coming from heaven. Everything in this moment was grand — the building, the statue, the priest, and then the choir. *Gloria in excelsis Deo!* My young mind was just boggled. My head kept bobbing back and forth from the statue to the priest to the choir. At the end of the mass, the priest stood there in front of us, raised his hands high, and blessed the assembly with a sign of the cross. My! I was so impressed by the majesty of the gesture that I left the church that day with the firm determination to become a priest. I remember all this vividly because as a boy I often stood on tall anthills in the pastures, stretching my arms and blessing my future imaginary congregations.

That is why, when I passed the national examination, I decided to sit for the Catholic Junior Seminary examination, and in October of 1970, I went to the seminary in Zaza, determined to fulfill my dream of becoming a priest. Mum bought the very simple equipment that was required — a bag, a blanket, and some other small things. Everything was soon ready, and I feverishly waited for the opening day for my new life in the seminary. Then on the departure day, in the morning, it suddenly dawned on me that I had no idea how to get to Zaza, having taken it for granted that Mum knew. But she did not. With some counsel from the neighbors, Mum accompanied me to the bus station in Gakenke to catch the bus to Rwamagana, where the road branched off to Zaza. The bus came, and before I knew what had happened, my courage had melted and I started crying like a child again.

I was twelve, and it was the first time I was going away from home, alone to an unfamiliar, unknown destination. Mum was embarrassed but was forced to climb into the bus with me to see me off to Rwamagana. Once in the bus, I met other students going to the same school. I was tremendously relieved to discover that I knew some of them. At Rwamagana, as we waited for the bus to Zaza, I began to notice that most of the new students were accompanied by their fathers or brothers. I was suddenly back in September 1965, my first day at primary school. *Karasira Petero Claver. Dead.* I remember standing on the side of the road, tears welling in my eyes. I looked aside and wiped my nose and my eyes, for deep inside, seeing those other children with their fathers had awakened my sad memories. In hindsight, I recognize that I was not the only one in that lonely situation; I was simply very sensitive to it, as every small incident during this time of transition seemed to remind me of the absence of my father.

Life in the seminary introduced me to a new kind of life on many levels. I was confident I was going to succeed, and I told myself I would be among the top-performing students just as I had always been. What I did not know was that all these other kids were also among the top students chosen from different schools. And some of them had a better understanding of secondary school life. The end of the first term brought me face to face with this new reality. When they proclaimed the term results, I was not first, nor second, nor even among the top ten of the class! I was 15th! In one way it was not a big issue since nobody knew me here or knew I had always been top of my class in primary school. Although my bubble of pride had burst, I decided to do something about it to regain my place. I managed to climb into fifth position and stayed there for most of the second year (like American 7th grade) and into third grade (like 8th grade). By the time we finished the first term of that year, the competition flywheel was in full gear, and I was already second of the class. I was quite satisfied with my progress. This was December 1972, and we got a break for Christmas vacation.

While the academic progress was gratifying and encouraging, my mum had helped us understand that this kind of success would not define us. She had brought us up to believe you can achieve well if you are ready to work hard and sweat for it. But success and achievement can be shared. Always aim higher and work harder for your goals, she taught, but never be bitter when somebody else gets more. "After all," she often said, "there is room for everybody in the world, and there is enough for all. The blessing of somebody else does not make you poorer." Or other principles, like "When your neighbor is blessed and becomes wealthy, do not be jealous; rejoice. If he does not help you, at least he will never steal from you." Be self-sacrificing and generous. Be honest and never win by cheating. "We are poor but we are not misers," she often repeated to us. "*Ubupfura buba mu nda*" (nobility is a matter of the heart). This concept of *ubupfura* or "nobility" was an integral part of who we were and were brought up to be. Aiming at the best in everything you did was part of *ubupfura*, at least how Mum saw it and taught it to us. I am often amazed at the pragmatic wisdom of life that our uneducated countryside mother tried to instill into her children. Each one of us bear something of that seal of hard work and dogged determination to do better in everything we do. My mother is now an old woman of 85, and I am still amazed at the kind of determination she has in life. All of us are now grown up and well established in our families. None have grown up to be a disappointment or a social liability.

Once we were back to school in January of 1973, rumors of trouble started circulating around us at the end of the first term. The Rwandan government was exchanging hard words with Burundi, our neighbor country to the south, and from that neighboring country, Hutu refugees had started trekking into Rwanda, recounting stories of cruelty and mass murders that the Tutsis in Burundi had committed against them. The rumors fueled a feeling of ethnic tension in the country. We had finished the first term without incident in the Southeast where our school was, not far from the border with Burundi, but already the rumors of trouble were spreading.

The second term started with bad news. We heard that in some schools in the central and southern provinces, Hutu students had attacked their Tutsi classmates and had even killed some. Hutu students in our school started forming cliques, and some even became verbally abusive against Tutsi students. News was coming that in all other schools, Tutsi students were being expelled, at times beaten and even killed in some places. In some areas, people arrived at their offices in the morning and found lists of Tutsi civil servants hanging on the doors, demanding that they leave and never return. In other areas, houses had been burnt and people killed. The authorities were denying these facts, but we knew it was a reality. Fear gripped us, and we lived waiting for the day when our turn would come to be asked to leave. In our school there was a large minority of Tutsi students, which I guess is why our classmates were hesitant to attack us. But the tension was growing everywhere — even in our seminary, the seedbed of future Catholic priests!

By the end of February, just one month back from the holidays, our school was closed. Bishop Joseph Sibomana, the leader of the Kibungo Diocese where our seminary was, came to our school and told us he had decided to close the school until further notice: "when things settle. I don't want violence and bloodshed in my school. All of you, Hutu, Tutsi, and whoever else you may think you are, go home." You could feel the anger and disappointment in his voice. As we all went, the Hutu students blamed us for spoiling their school year!

By the time I got home, things had gone sour even in the village, and the atmosphere was visibly tense. One of our neighbors who had been friends with my father called me and explained to me what was brewing in the village. "They are ready to attack and wipe us out any time. They are just waiting for a signal from the authorities. And we do not stand any chance of surviving this time." He also told me that they would not even spare women or children as they had in the past. He then said he was "determined to stand his ground. I'm ready to die but many of them will die with me." He disclosed to me that he was determined to defend his compound, using arrows and his bow.

I thought his plan was good, but I never told him I was going to follow his lead and prepare myself for any possibility. In my youthful anger, I took his warning seriously and started training with my father's bow and arrows. In the past, every man had his spear, a bow, and arrows. Although these traditional weapons were not used except in areas where they did hunting, it was part of the culture and the normal set up of a house. I was determined I would never just sit there, waiting to be bludgeoned into pulp. "We will die, yes, but many of them will go into death with us," the voice of the old man kept echoing in my head.

I started spending sleepless nights, just waiting to hear if anything would happen under the night's inky cloak. Mum never knew why I was always behind the compound repeatedly shooting at targets with the bow and the arrows, two hours every day, and at times more. She probably thought it was a new youthful fancy from school and never suspected what my 15-year-old mind was planning as a solution to our dilemma. My hands had grown callous through the repeated shooting, but at the end of one month, I had acquired so much skill I could shoot far and precisely. "Yes, we will die but many will die with us," went my mantra. But nothing happened, and the tensions seemed to die down! By April we were called back to school.

Just two weeks back into school, the worst happened. Our school was attacked by Hutu students from The Teacher Training School in connivance with some of the students in our community. Fortunately, they were not well prepared, and we all fled our attackers, Hutus and Tutsis alike. Our fear was great, but all the time I kept regretting that this was happening far away from my bow and my arrows. What a good game they would have made in that mass crowd when they were coming! But this time I was running; it was a matter of getting as far as we could from the attackers. Later in the evening we came back when things had quieted and the attackers had gone back to their school. But life was never to be the same, as the Hutu students had understood the message and were determined to do as everybody else was doing! Tutsis had to go and our turn came. The tension in the school never subsided, and one week after that,

45

we were asked to leave. Although the Hutu students did not dare attack us in front of the watching school officials, they did taunt us — sneering and jeering. We kept our cool and decided to go, but we refused to let them treat us however they wanted. I was weeping inside that I did not have my bow and arrows. I remember leaving our classroom with hands full of my notebooks, anger in my heart, and tears running down my cheeks. One of my friends saw the tears and thought I was being a coward. He put down his books and gave me a powerful slap on the cheek. "You coward," he said, "straighten up and leave this place with your head high. This is not the place nor the time to show your emotions; be a man." He did not know how much determination was in those tears, but his slap boosted my determination. This was the time to be a man!

We left the school early in the morning on board three school pick-up trucks. These were our terms: we did not want to leave in separate groups in fear that those who stayed behind or those who went ahead in small numbers would be attacked. By the time we were well on our way along the road, we were met by Bishop Joseph Sibomana in his car with two military lorries full of soldiers behind him. He ordered our convoy to turn back and follow him. Many of us did not like the idea, but we had to obey. The Hutu students had resumed normal life, peeling the bananas for lunch and cleaning the school classes and dorms as usual. All of a sudden, they saw our three pick-ups coming back, with the bishop and the escort of soldiers. A school assembly was hurriedly called, and we were broken into two groups — the Tutsi students into the school cafeteria and the Hutu students into one of the large classes.

The teachers and the bishop went for a meeting to decide what to do in the circumstance. By two o'clock the meeting was over, and we were called into the school central compound for another assembly. The Bishop harangued us, expressing his great disappointment to see that people who were training to become the future clergy of the nation would engage in such disreputable behavior. At the end of his speech, he read the names of students who would be expelled from the school, singled out by the school authorities as leaders on both sides of the trouble. "This," he said, "is a warning. Any new trouble and I will close the school." Then he called each class, while the military officer called two armed soldiers to go with them. The soldiers ended up staying with us for two months, until July of 1973

46

when General Juvenal Habyarimana overthrew President Kayibanda. The soldiers doggedly followed us wherever we went, always sitting behind us in class, in the school cafeteria, and even in church.

There was apparent peace in the school, but deep inside we knew the Hutus were simmering with hatred and disappointment at their failed attempt, and we were seething with fear and anger. Threats, insinuations, insults kept coming our way, but we clinched our teeth and held our ground until the end. By this time, my mind was firmly made up that all Hutus were bad. My internal monologue continually ran: "They killed our fathers under the pretext they were accomplices of the Tutsi refugees (*Inyenzi*), but what reason can they give us now? These students do not even know me. I have never offended any of them, so why would they want to kill me?" And the conclusion always came clear and unambiguous: "They are simply bad and wicked from the core, born murderers!" And that feeling sank into my heart with the weight of an anchor from the trauma we had to endure all those months. I had survived again; I had lived up to my name, Rutayisire. Death had not taken me, but my heart was filling up with hatred for the Hutus.

Chapter Four

HIGHER AND DEEPER

"See to it that no bitter root grows up to cause trouble and defile many"
Hebrews 12:15

THE NEXT FOUR YEARS in the junior seminary passed without any major incident, but the questions never left my mind. Why do they do this to us? We lived with a feeling of uncertainty and threat looming over our future, not knowing if it was over or if it was going to come back again. Government policies on access to education started getting tougher and tougher on the Tutsis — but soon policies also negatively affected Hutus from regions other than the Northwest where most of the political leaders came from. Before long, government and media spoke like it was a favor for the Tutsi to live in Rwanda at all. There was not an obvious threat to our lives, but who would enjoy living in a place where you are treated like a second-class citizen in your own motherland?

I definitely resented the restrictive policies, and I always hated any reference to the Tutsi as being an ethnic minority. There was an unrelenting set of messages reminding me that I was not at home in my native land. This feeling dampened my enthusiasm for hard work at school during the remaining years of secondary school life. As I often told myself, "Why toil so much when there is no future in this land?" Deep inside I knew I could have done better, but I could not see any reason. Despite all the discouragement, I managed to stay in the second position in our class until graduation, not out of enthusiasm but out of pride. I comforted myself that at least I knew I could beat them in school, and that in itself gave me a certain feeling of achievement. I always hid my dark sentiments with a posture of silence and distance, which some took for timidity and others for arrogance.

By the time I graduated from the junior seminary in 1977, I had grown out of my ambition to become a priest, so I applied to go to university. I have to be honest and say that what we had gone through did not have any influence on my decision. I simply felt that being a priest was not my calling. The sad thing was, at this junction of my life, I had lost any sense of ambition and was just drifting through life in frustration and uncertainty because I had made up my mind there was no good future for a Tutsi in Rwanda. As I look back, I can say there is hardly any worse situation to be in than to live with a heart emptied of good plans for the future, just drifting through life like a tree thrown into the current of a river.

By then the government policies on education were becoming more and more restrictive on the Tutsi, and getting a scholarship would be shocking stroke of luck. The day I took my application documents to the Ministry of Education confirmed my fears that I did not stand any chance of getting a place at the university. I went into the Scholarships Office trembling with fear and apprehension, friends having told me that the woman in charge was very rude and ill-tempered. And there she was, sitting motionless like a statue. She took my papers and checked them one by one, reading every line like a student working on a hard examination paper. Then she got to my identification papers! She took her eyes from the papers, looked at me intently, and abruptly threw my papers to the ground with an "ugh" sound of disgust. I stood there, dumbfounded, wondering what crime my identity had committed to be treated with such contempt. I was transfixed into a pillar of confused emotions, seething anger mixed with bewilderment. I did not know what to say or do, but deep inside I felt like strangling the woman or spitting in her face. I swallowed my disgust and refrained from any gesture or word.

As if the insult was not enough, she turned towards me and spurted out in her coarse voice: "Get going, don't you see we are busy and have other things to attend to?" I left the place, tears blurring my vision as they always did every time I was angry. I stood in front of the door, recomposed myself, and went out as if nothing had happened. But deep down inside I was deeply hurt. All the way home I sat silent in the bus, ruminating the misery of living in a country that does not give you hope for the future when you are young. There is no worse curse for a human being than to live a life that does not allow you to dream of a better tomorrow.

When the University opened, I was stunned to hear my name called on the radio among those who had received a government scholarship, which was important because in our system only those who had received such scholarships could attend. The names of the lucky candidates were always read publicly on the national radio station. Back then there was only one University, and it accommodated only a small number of students. The first-year students were so few that their list was always read after the news on the national radio as a brief announcement. For three whole months I had been sitting home, despairing for my future, and this news came as a ray of hope, a rescue rope to haul me out of the deep pit of discouragement.

My five years at the University passed without much trouble. Small incidents regularly popped up to remind us that the ethnic sword of Damocles was still dangling over our heads, like during an aborted coup in 1980 when we were almost expelled from school again. Aggression against Tutsi students at the University was supposed to spark off a wave of massacres and expulsions and then other schools would have followed — as in 1973 — but the plan was nipped in the bud, and nothing happened. And there were always slurs of graffiti on the notice boards, innuendos in conversations, and constant moments of awkwardness to remind you that the fire of ethnic hatred was not totally out. But all in all, life was bearable.

I was doing well in sports, running 400m for the University track and field team, and I was getting good grades in all my classes. I had set the bar high for myself, determined to pass each course with a mark of distinction. I enjoyed the limelight of success in the five years of life at the University, and by the time we were graduating, the new policy was that the University would start recruiting high-achieving students to become Assistant Professors in order to gradually create a faculty of Rwandan nationals. At that time, most of the lecturers at the National University of

Rwanda were expatriates. A gleam of hope was kindled in my heart, and I urged myself to aim for the highest marks, just in case they made comparisons during the recruitment.

And I made it, finishing my final year with the highest grade in the class, a "High Distinction"! I did indeed get my position with the University, and that very first year I started charting my path to the top. I have never dreamed of becoming a politician, but teaching was always my ambition. I wanted to become a great university professor, writing books and teaching with excellence. I began preparing articles in literature, and I even started researching for a future doctoral thesis, although it was going to take at least four years for me to be on the University faculty before beginning it. But better to start early if you are going to achieve outstanding results, as I had learned from my previous thesis. *Akabando k'iminsi gacibwa kare, kakabikwa kure*, "The stick you will use when you are old is cut early in life and kept in a safe place." This was one of my mother's favorite sayings. I started warming up inside, feeling I had finally found a niche and could make my life here. In the face of my hope, the policies were still getting worse and worse against the Tutsis: the "equilibre ethnique" (ethnic quota) was now accepted as a law in the Constitution, and very few Tutsis were allowed in positions of influence, be it in Government institutions and even churches. But as before, I had lived up to my name and almost survived even the ethnic equilibrium! Rutayisire, "if death does not take him. . . ."

Then out of nowhere came a big blow, like thunder in a blue summer sky! A friend called me one morning from the Ministry of Labor to tell me he had seen an appointment letter sending me into a secondary school rather than the University. I told him it must have been a mistake, but he seemed to know more and advised me to start lobbying to get things sorted out. "If you have some contacts, ask them to look into this for you; otherwise, it is more serious than you think." I started running here and there to find out what had gone wrong. The University authorities stood by me and wrote recommendation letters praising my good performance. That didn't work. Somewhere up there, somebody was blocking the process, and my last hopes were dashed to pieces the day I went to see the Director General in charge of Higher Education. I went to see him, deluding myself that he was an acquaintance and thus would be my ally in the matter. After all, everywhere I went everybody was telling me it was a simple administrative mistake that would be corrected without much ado.

It took me some time of waiting to get the appointment, but I was finally able to explain my case, showing him all the literature of recommendation from the Department, the Chancellery, and even reminding him we had often worked together. He sat there listening, and the kind of attention he gave me rekindled some hope that a good answer was coming. Finally, though, his fatal cryptic answer came: "I thought you were smart! Don't you understand there is no way you will get back into the Faculty?" Then I went back into more explanations, hoping to placate him into some understanding. I could sense he was getting impatient, and he finally cut me short and concluded, "If you were smart enough, you would understand your demotion came from the Office of the President, and there must be a good reason for the decision." He said it so matter-of-factly, as if it were an accepted truth, as if I was stupid not to know it. "There must be a good reason." "If you were smart enough." I sat there, dumbfounded, anger boiling in my heart, tears welling up in my eyes.

In a moment my whole life reeled in a slow backward motion; then very fast it swung back into the present. *1983, 1973, 1963 . . . 1973, 1983!* My mind was now going faster. I could feel my heart pumping, my temples were becoming tense, and some veins must have started showing on my face — anger, deadly youthful anger. My hands were wet with moisture, and I held both sides of my chair to stay calm. Yes, 1963: my father. 1973: my friends. 1983: me, my job! Something ugly, something bad has to happen against us every ten years! Yes, there must be a reason! I stood up, looked the man in the eye and said, "Merci Monsieur le Directeur General," with my teeth clinched. If I had had a knife in my pocket that day, I think I would have stabbed the man to death. I turned around, dashed out of the office, and slammed the door behind me with all my strength, the only outlet left for my murderous mood. That was August 1983.

I went home and for three whole months I was heartsick with bitter disappointment. If somebody had come around recruiting a rebel army to fight the system in place, I would have been an easy recruit. Day and night I was there, gnashing my teeth, brooding over my past and dreaming of a free nation where people would live without injustice and oppression. I had learned from my mother never to wallow in self-commiseration, never to let any problem overwhelm me into defeat, to always look for a solution. But I knew there was no solution here; this was not a personal problem. This was a system, a rotten system too big for any individual to change or even to challenge on his own. I knew there was nothing I could do and that helplessness in itself made my heart sick. I have often reflected, *This is how people grow into rebels, terrorists, or suicide bombers.* They are tired of a system, fed up with simply surviving in hopelessness. They do not hate individuals; they hate the system and anybody associated with it. And such characters grow aplenty in the fertile soil of dead hopes crushed under the weight of unjust and oppressive systems. Oh, how my heart cries for those children born in refugee settlements all over the world, those places that do not offer hope and space to dream of a better future. My heart weeps for those many others, born in the ghetto shanty towns of giant cities or into bonded labor, or in war-torn nations where hatred is passed on like a deadly legacy. I still rebel whenever I see injustice and misery, and my heart always goes to the victims and the underprivileged! May I never be reconciled with injustice.

By November, all the money I had from my last university paycheck was almost finished, and need brought me back to my senses. I decided to pick up the pieces of my broken dreams and carry on with life. I went back to the Ministry of Education to find out which secondary school they had sent me to. This is how I started my new life in the remote Rulindo Girls High School.

Chapter Five

OUT OF THE ABYSS

"Out of the depths I cry to you, O Lord;
O Lord, hear my voice.
Let your ears be attentive to my cry for mercy"
Psalm 130:1-2

EVERYTHING ABOUT RULINDO made me feel like I had been sent
into exile. Rulindo is set atop a very steep hill, and in 1983 it was not easy
to get there. The public bus went there once a week, always crammed full
with passengers carrying all types of goods, foods, and smells. The road
was bad and dusty. For me, climbing Rulindo hill was another Calvary.
On my way up, I passed through the eucalyptus forest on the brow of the
hill, and at the top I sat down in the shade of a big tree to rest. Its trunk
was knotted and very contorted. Its branches were crooked and shriveled,
while all the other trees around it were tall and straight. The shape of the
tree intrigued me, and I felt a strange attachment and sympathy for it. I
started wondering what had made it so crooked and so scarred! Its past
must have been very difficult. *Maybe that's how I look inside?* I wondered
to myself.

The living conditions in Rulindo left much to be desired. There
was no housing for the teachers, and for the first week while I was searching for accommodation, I had to sleep with a friend in his small room,

sharing the same bed in a house he shared with three other teachers. Coming from my comfortable, fully-furnished university house to live in these conditions added to my depression. Most of the teachers were also disgruntled, and the general atmosphere did not offer anything to boost my depleted morale. I started going out with colleagues, drowning our misery in alcohol through most of the hours of the evening. I always found drinking to be the most boring pastime. The influence of a mother who never drank and who always discouraged us from drinking, the disciplined life of a junior seminary, and the self-discipline of a 400m runner had all contributed to making me very reserved with alcohol. I eventually decided to quit the drinking; instead, I isolated myself in reading.

My behavior at the school was no doubt enigmatic to my colleagues. I was obnoxious toward the school headmistress. The first day I met her, I immediately spotted her as the right scapegoat for the system I hated. After all, she was the head of the school, and in my eyes she was the representative of the government that had deprived me of my rights. The first months I made hell for her. On one occasion I purposefully decided to humiliate her in the presence of other teachers when she asked to see my preparation notebook.

"Look sister," I told her, "if you do not have other useful things to do, take a break. I teach English, and you don't even understand one word of that language, so how can you pretend to evaluate what I do?" Other teachers did not like her either, some because of her behavior and others because of the general discontent they brought to that isolated place. That day they all reveled in seeing her humiliation and embarrassment.

She tried to remind me she was doing her job, but I retorted, "I have other things to do. If you are not satisfied with my performance, just write and send me back to the Ministry of Education. That way you will be rid of my presence and I'll be saved from this horrible place."

Everything I was saying was quite true, but deep inside I knew my behavior was wrong. Despite my anger, I had not yet lost my sense of values, and I recognized I had started living in contradiction with my real self. Human behavior, contrary to what many tend to think, is dominated by emotions and not by reason. And in its irrationality, the wounded heart breeds irrational behaviors that it justifies by past victimization. Victims tend to create more victims around them. I always appeared joyful and positive in the classroom, but once outside, my dark mood would take over, enveloping me like a wet cloak. I often stood in front of the teachers' room, my back against the wall, fixing a blank gaze into the distance and brooding over my misery. How can I get out of this? How will our people get out of this injustice? Although I always thought about my predicament, I knew the only solution would be a total overhaul of the whole system. But there was no way out. And that was the source of my despair. The students were puzzled by my changing moods, and they nicknamed me "Question Mark." For them I was an enigma. A 25-year-old graduate from the university, a very good teacher, jovial in class but very dark outside. I never told anybody what had transpired to land me in Rulindo, and everybody was trying to find a reason that would explain my odd behavior.

Out of boredom I started reading the Bible. As I read, I discovered very interesting truths about life in general and about myself in particular. I liked the way God hates injustice. Although I had done my studies in a Roman Catholic junior seminary, I had never until recently owned a Bible (the one I was reading was a Christmas gift from a friend), and I had never been encouraged to read it beyond the texts we were studying.

I thought I knew quite a bit about the Bible: when it was written, how and by whom and other such peripheral details, but I had never taken time to read it thoroughly. It was a great challenge to discover how little I knew about this book that I had often criticized as full of contradictions and inconsistencies, simply parroting what I had read or heard from other people. I had always admired the character of Jesus but had never thought of him as an example for my own life: after all he was God and could do and say what he said because of that advantage. My attention was first held by Paul, who fascinated me. He was forceful in his speeches, articulate in his reasoning, and determined in his actions. I have always been enthralled by the biographies of great people (good and bad!). I always read about the lives and sayings of great characters because I wanted to find out what had shaped them and how I could recreate these things in my own life. I liked Paul immediately.

One day, when I was reading his letter to the Philippians, the verse "for me to live is Christ and to die is gain" (1:21) jumped off the page and gripped me in a special way — a definition of life. That was what I was looking for, something worth living for, something to even die for. For

Paul, living was Christ. What is my definition of life? What do I live for? I was struck that my life had no definition. I was just drifting through the days, mourning my dreary existence. Then out of nowhere came the question, "Where is Christ in your life?" To be honest, that was a question I had never been asked; I had never even thought it could be a question. Here I was, a Christian, going to church on Sundays (when there was nothing more appealing to do, I have to confess) but without any room for Christ in my life. "It is inconsistent and dishonest," I told myself, "to call yourself a Christian when there is no room for Christ in your life."

As a result of this reflection, I made an honest decision and stopped going to church. That key decision slowly snowballed into an avalanche of questions: "What reason will you then give to people for not going to church? Will you tell them there is no God?" And other such questions. For sure, I knew there was a God. I had seen his hand on many occasions, and there was no way I was going to deny his existence. I finally decided to read the Bible three times from cover to cover (a reading practice I had acquired through my academic training) before making a final decision regarding my predicament. I prepared some good academic questions for my reading: What is the major theme of the book? Is it coherent? Is it cohesive? Then I gave myself a deadline of six months to have gone through the book three times.

By the time I finished my assignment, I had made up my mind to live according to the book — calling right what it calls right and calling wrong what it calls wrong. I discovered what I had been looking for, a standard and a reference for my behavior. Then I wrote to my friends about my new findings and decision, telling them I was now determined to live according to the Bible, calling right what it calls right and wrong what it calls wrong. Many were astounded to hear my determination, others thought it was just a temporary tantrum to relieve myself from the disappointment of having lost my good job. Some went into mourning! At the time I did not know the Christian jargon of "saved," "born again," "converted," or the many complicated words I would discover later. I had simply found a lifestyle—a reference for judging my behavior — and that was enough. The more I aligned my life with my new convictions, the more I started sloughing off the thought, speech, behavior, and habits that had often given me deep feelings of guilt. My relationships started brightening with people around me, and a new sense of emotional release was developing in my life. Michel Kayitaba was a born-again teacher at the school, and I started going to his home, eager to share with him the joys of my new spiritual discoveries. Michel is a very good listener, and I often think that's what I needed: somebody to listen to me as I was putting into words my new mindset.

Reading the Bible became like an addiction for me. I would read during all my free hours; I traveled with it on the bus and sat late at night devouring it. I was fascinated by the people and their behavior. Most of the stories were familiar from the seven years at the seminary, but the application to daily life was new to me. Every good behavior highlighted a shortcoming in my life and became a request in prayer. I often found myself writing in the margins of my Bible, "Lord, purify me like you purified this leper"; "Lord, make me as determined as Daniel was when he decided not to defile himself"; "God, make me like Joseph when he was in temptation"; "Lord, use me like you used Moses"; and other such short prayers. This habit has actually stayed with me even today. This personalized way of reading acknowledges the living nature of the Bible and makes it more refreshing and meaningful.

During my years at the junior seminary, the Stations of the Cross during Lent before Easter had always been my favorite. There was something powerful and mysteriously engaging that always gripped my heart and brought tears to my eyes when they read the stories of Jesus going to the cross. I often sat there in the church, my heart overwhelmed by feelings of gratitude, wondering what I could do in return for what Jesus had done for me on that tree. But nobody ever told me, and I always thought I was just being sentimental. When I started reading the Bible, I often went back to the cross stories and would again and again be overwhelmed by the same feeling of gratitude and dedication, but more powerfully this time because I knew what it meant and what God expected from me. I often sat in my room, reading my Bible, singing hymns about the cross, and finishing in a prayer of dedication.

Even today, more than thirty years after my conversion, the cross still has that same unfathomable power over my heart and my whole life. In my reading habits, there are times when I allow my mind to wander, so that I hop inside the story; rather than being merely a reader, I become a participant. One day I did this when I was reading Jesus's journey to the cross, and that turned my whole life upside down! I jumped into the moment when Jesus was going up to Jerusalem, and I became part of the great crowd that went before him chanting, "Hosanna, hosanna, the one who comes in the Name of the Lord." I am now part of the crowd, brandishing my palm branch, singing my gratitude at the top of my voice. Then all of a sudden, the crowd disappears and Jesus's entourage dwindles down to the twelve apostles. Our noise is over, the singing has stopped, and the euphoria of the day dies off as all disperse to the four corners of the city. Jesus is now in the upper room with just his twelve disciples. The whole atmosphere is strangely sober, and he is telling them a sad story. I am eavesdropping on their conversation from outside. Then one of them leaves. The company dwindles, and they squeeze to fill the empty space left. Hours later, Judas is back, with the mob. This time they are not chanting "hosanna" but just "get him," "don't allow him to escape." He surrenders to them but calmly pleads to let his company go. His friends disappear; nine run away and abandon him. Peter follows from a distance and John is still close by. I follow from a distance, silent, incognito in the crowd, bewildered. Insults, slapping, fists, sticks, nothing is spared.

My mind flashes back to 1963! I see my father surrounded by the mob; I now don't know where I am. My anger is gaining momentum at every step. By the time we reach the cross, I am in a fury and words escape from my mouth, loud, audible: "These Hutus! How long will they do this to innocent people?" I cried out. All of a sudden I am back to my senses and remember this is not Rwanda, but Judea! I read on but deep inside me something has happened, and I am unable to keep my distance from the story anymore. When Jesus cries out, "Father, forgive them for they do not know what they are doing," I again loudly exclaim, "No!"

"No, no, no...you cannot pray like that for these unfaithful people. Lord, how do you dare pray like that for these people? When they were hungry you fed them, when they were sick, you healed them, and when their children were dead, you raised them. And here they are chanting, "crucify him," sneering and insulting, repaying evil for good? How do you dare? You should curse them."

My internal dialogue went on like that: a look back at what Jesus had done for them, a look at what they were doing to him, then my suggestion as to what he should have said (what I would have said if I were in his place). I could bear it no longer. I stopped my reading and said, "God, I hope you are not telling me to do the same with the Hutus. Forget it." I had now reached an area of life where I totally disagreed with Jesus, and that was very disturbing. I stopped my reading and went out for a walk. I passed the shriveled tree, still meditating on that prayer from the cross: *Father, forgive them.*

"No, Lord, you do not expect me to forgive these people what they have done. I will follow you, always, everywhere, but let me take a different path on this issue. I can't forgive them." For two weeks or more (I don't really remember, having never kept a journal), my heart was wrestling with God about this. Then I finally gave in. I took a day off from the school and stayed home to sort out my heart problem with God.

That morning I took my Bible and read through all the passages talking about our enemies and how to treat them. Again, I found the Bible very cohesive and coherent on this topic. I read about Moses praying for his sister who was punished with leprosy for speaking against him. I read about Joseph hugging his brothers, weeping over their wickedness and calling them to get closer to him, amidst the Egyptians to whom they had sold him. I read about the different commandments to love our enemies. I read about Jesus praying for his tormentors on the cross, about Stephen praying for those who stoned him, and Paul praying for those who abandoned him when he went for his trial. I was deeply convicted and ultimately convinced that I should forgive. For a true Christian, forgiveness is not an option, it is an order. And it is to your advantage.

When you do not forgive, you remain chained to your past experiences, a victim forever. At that time I did not know why God would expect such a difficult thing from us. I did repent of my anger and my bitterness, and that I had even hated innocent people for nothing. Then I made a long list of people I hated with cause — those who had beaten my father, the *bourgemestre* who had ordered him shot, our schoolmates of 1973, the woman in the Scholarship Office, the Director General in the Ministry of Higher Education, and many others I could remember who had had a role in wounding my heart.

I turned to God and prayed, "Lord, it is difficult for me to forgive these people, but give me the grace to let go." Then I just pronounced the forgiveness. "Lord, I forgive them." But deep inside I was still struggling with my heart. *God, why didn't you leave us a way to hate those who are so difficult to forgive?* I kept asking. Then I was reminded of Jesus's prayer, "Father, forgive them." It was when it was the most difficult to forgive that Jesus prayed that prayer: when his head was crowned with thorns, when his hands and feet were fastened to the tree with nails, when his whole body was bleeding, when everybody around him was jeering. And he looked down at that mob of ungrateful faces and prayed, "Father, forgive them." It was very powerful, even overwhelming to think about that act. He did not wait for the third day and the victory of the resurrection, but he forgave when he was still suffering. I was totally disarmed. When you hear Jesus hanging on the cross and praying for his enemies, all your defenses are swept away. What other reason can you find to justify your unforgiving behavior when you claim to be the follower of such a King?

The most difficult exercise for me was next, to "pray for your enemies and bless them." My heart could not obey. I opened my mouth, but it was as if something inside me was saying, "No, curse them." Then all of a sudden, with what must surely have been the empowering grace of God, I broke into tears and wept as I prayed for each of them, one by one, calling all types of blessing upon them: "God, bless this one, bless his family, bless his business and all . . . ." By the time I finished praying through my list of unforgivables, I was totally exhausted and took a long nap. I woke up late in the evening, and it was as if a heavy burden had been lifted off my heart. I felt light like a feather, and my heart was overflowing with a deep feeling of peace and joy.

I decided that every time I remembered what the Hutus have done to us, I would bless them. And this happened often, even after my conversion. I have heard many people saying that "when you come to Christ, you are a new creation and the old is gone," as if your awakened soul means wounds and bitterness will just disappear from your heart and mind. In my experience, it is not so simple or immediate. By the time I came to this release of bitterness, I had been preaching the gospel for three years, but my wounds were still hidden and dormant deep inside, like a deposit of mud at the bottom of a pond. On the surface the water appears delusively clear and beautiful, but deep down the mud is still there, and when stirred up, the water clouds and discolors. Over time, the more I prayed for the people, the more I was healed, and that is when I stopped feeling the pain from their offenses. My wounds improved slowly, and they finally healed.

It took me years to be able to share this experience because I was afraid people would not understand. I had never even heard anyone give such a testimony, although I knew deep inside many people were hurting with similar unaddressed wounds that had never been cleansed or bandaged. It seemed as if talking about the injustices or wounds of our history was taboo. I remember one day, in a moment of excitement in the middle of a sermon, I forgot about this unspoken prohibition and gave the testimony as I preached. Some friends later discreetly approached me to warn me: "Such testimonies are dangerous and will get you in trouble with the powers that be. More than that, your testimony made many people ill at ease."

And that was the game of the church — everyone played it safe. I fell silent and filed away the experience. I healed and forgave the offenses, but deep inside I could not bring myself to accept the injustices of the system, even the injustice of not being free to publicly declare forgiveness. Forgiveness does not mean acceptance of the unacceptable. Injustice in whatever form will always remain unacceptable to me.

Life in Rulindo improved, and I even started to love it. I had found a new reason for living, and my enthusiasm was back with all the optimism of youth. My nickname, "Mr. Question Mark," disappeared along with my melancholy. I started building relationships with my colleagues. I even went to the headmistress, confessed my past misbehaviors to her and asked for her forgiveness. She was deeply moved when she heard my story, and from that day on we became very good friends. During that time, the Literature and Linguistics Department at the National University was still pressing hard to see if I could resume my position at the University, but nothing came to fruition. The Ministry of Education was adamant, and we finally agreed to give up. But God was opening another door to comfort my heart. That was 1985.

The British Council had given scholarships for English teachers in secondary schools to train for six months in the UK. After the proficiency tests, the examiner called me and asked me if I was ready to serve as a "guinea pig" for a full Master's degree.

"I have been impressed by your performance in the tests, and I'd like to give you a chance. At the same time, we will see if students from the Rwanda University can go through a crash Master's course in a British university. If you fail, you will have received better training than the others who are going to stay for only six months; if you succeed, you will get your degree. Either way, you lose nothing. And I will make sure nobody in the Ministry of Education discovers that you are going for a Master's. You will go like the others but simply to a different university and for a different length of time."

Challenges have always motivated me, and I gladly accepted. This time the system did not block my path despite one individual delaying me, hoping for a bribe that he never got. I went to the University College of North Wales in Bangor, and twelve months later I came back with my Master's Degree in Applied Linguistics. Although I entertained quiet hopes of returning to a faculty position at the University, again I ended up in Rulindo School. This time it did not affect me because I had not allowed my heart to dream too much about the possibility. After all, this was clearly not a matter of competency or credentials. I went back to work with extra zeal, committed to giving the best to my students.

Life in Bangor had strengthened my faith and opened my horizons; it had even made me cherish my teaching profession. Here, teaching is a well-respected profession; at least that was a value instilled in us in the courses we took. One of our lecturers used to insist that a language teacher finds his joy in taking a student from a level of zero linguistic ability to a level of language fluency and easy communication. That became my motto and my joy.

Despite the government opposition to my getting back onto the faculty at the National University, I became a regular visiting lecturer in the English Department. That gave me some extra income and alleviated the sense of loss I still felt in my heart. Rulindo was slowly becoming an enjoyable place to live! During the cold mornings, the valley below Rulindo hill would be shrouded in white fog, and you could not guess the sun was already shining on the top of the hill. When you climbed the hill, you would leave the fog behind in the valley and find yourself in the warmth of the sunny air on the top. And that is how I started viewing my life: from the damp cold fog of my past, God was taking me to the bright sunny top of the hill.

Chapter Six

TESTED BY FIRE

"He ordered the furnace heated seven times hotter than usual"
Daniel 3:19

I LEFT RULINDO at the end of the school year in July 1990 to pioneer a Christian work among the university students with the Groupes Bibliques Universitaires, a branch of the International Fellowship of Evangelical Students (IFES). In the United States, the branch of IFES is called Inter-Varsity Christian Fellowship. To avoid complications, I resigned from government services, which meant I would never work in a government position again. I got married on August 18, 1990, and less than two months later, on October 1, the Rwanda Patriotic Front (RPF) attacked Rwanda from Kagitumba, on the border with Uganda. As explained in the Preface, this Rwanda Patriotic Front was a political movement born in the refugee settlements, and it came with a military wing called the Rwanda Patriotic Army (RPA). Mainly composed of young Tutsi leaders who grew up in exile with the frustration of being refugees in countries that neighbor their motherland, the RPF had an attractive agenda of bringing home all the refugees but also creating a nation where all Rwandans would be equal and would enjoy the same rights. No wonder this attracted many sympathizers, mainly among the young Tutsis inside the country who had been living in the kind of frustrating environment I have described thus far.

At first it only seemed to be a rumor, but by midday it was confirmed by international radio that a group of armed Tutsis had attacked the country. The Rwanda national radio station later gave a different version of the incident, announcing that a "group of Ugandan army soldiers" invaded Rwanda by the Kagitumba border but that "the situation was under control."

The invasion sparked hellfire against the Tutsis inside the country. From that Monday October 1, the tension kept mounting. The whole night of Thursday, October 4, Kigali City thundered with the noise of heavy artillery and machine guns. Nobody knew what had happened and what was going on; we all thought the RPA was already in town. I eventually dared to look out through the window, and after some close observation, I told Penina, my wife, "You know, I don't know what it is but this is not war. All the bullets are going up as if they were shooting down planes, but there are no planes in the sky! I suppose the army is either making a mock attack to desensitize the population to war, or they are just exercising to protect the city." After my conclusion, I slipped into bed and went to sleep again.

The following morning the shooting had totally died off, and I told Penina again, "This is more proof it was not a war. You do not fight during the night and stop in the morning; we should at least be hearing some sporadic shootings here and there in different parts of the city. Let's wait and see." The National radio station gave a very disturbing report in the morning news, saying that the enemy had attacked the city during the night but that the situation was again under control. Through the same communiqué, everybody was officially requested to stay home to allow the authorities and the security services to clean the city before life could resume. Deep inside, my intuition told me there was a nasty plot afoot, but I could not tell what. We spent the whole day inside, going out occasionally just to warm up in the sun. Only military vehicles were moving, and the city looked dead. After lunch I decided to take a nap.

No sooner had I started sleeping than I was awakened by a loud noise, and I opened my eyes to find myself face to face with three soldiers in combat uniforms, pointing their guns at my chest. I pretended to be half asleep and then lazily said, "What is happening?"

"Hands up, and quick! Do not move," one of the soldiers ordered. "How many *Inyenzi* are you hiding here?" he asked. The dehumanizing term *inyenzi* (cockroaches) had again become standard. Adopted from the earlier years of persecution, it was being reapplied to the RPA soldiers who would attack at night and were invisible in day time. Soon, it became the normal derogative term for all the Tutsis and was intensively used in the propaganda for the genocide.

"None. There is nobody else except me, my wife, and our houseboy," I told him.

"Where are the people who spent the night here?" he inquired.

"We are all here; there was nobody else who spent the night here," I answered. One of the soldiers kept us at gun-point while the other was searching under the bed and in the cupboard. The one who seemed to be their leader was checking the books and the papers that were on the night table.

Then he came to my passport. "Why do you have a passport?" he asked. I was puzzled by the stupid question but decided to answer as innocently as I could.

"Last month I went to Lome in Togo, and I needed a passport to travel."

"I see you have gone through Nairobi, who were you meeting there?"

Again that sounded very stupid, but I had decided to remain cool and innocent.

"I did not meet anybody except the passengers who were on the same flight and the hotel people where I spent the night. Otherwise I did not have any business in Nairobi except catching my connection the following day."

"You are lying."

That took me by surprise, but I remained composed and told him, "I serve God, and it is him I take as my witness that what I told you is the whole truth."

"Do you know a certain Mastajabu?" he asked again, out of nowhere.

"Yes, I know him, he is the one who sold me this house," I answered.

"Then you know where he lives?"

"Yes, I do," I answered.

"Then put on your shirt and let's go; lead us to his place," he commanded.

It was becoming very tense, and I did not know what to do. I hurriedly put on a shirt, and when I wanted to comb my hair, he pushed me rudely:

"Get going, who said you are going out for a feast?"

I went out in the front and all three men followed me, pointing their guns at my back. Outside the house four other soldiers were positioned in the four corners of the compound, fingers on their triggers as if expecting an attack any moment. It was horribly terrifying! My heart was beating fast, sweat was running under my arms, and my throat became dry. We went in total silence, only the heavy thumping of the military boots on the dirt could be heard. Our neighbors were looking through their windows but without any noise, motionless like dummies in the windows of a commercial street. We reached the place where they had parked their lorry, and we climbed on board. Some other civilians were already in there, surrounded by menacing armed soldiers. Until then, I had not understood what was happening. Everybody was silent, and we were not talking to each other. Some of the other civilians, at close look, had stripes on their cheeks as if they had been slapped, and one had swollen lips and was dirty as if he had been beaten and dragged in the dust. I found I was lucky they had not assaulted me. When we got to Mastajabu's place, I climbed down and went with the same seven soldiers who had been at my place.

Four of them took the same positions in the four corners of the compound, and the three who had been inside my house remained. Then the one who acted like their commander turned to me and said, "Run, and let me not see you again."

He did not have to tell me a second time. I dashed out of the compound like a bird escaping from the trap of a fowler. I slowed down past the lorry, and those who were inside seemed surprised to see me going. "Eh, you there, come back here," shouted one of the soldiers. "Who told you to go?" he asked when I got closer.

"The Commander," I answered. He did not seem convinced but he finally said, "Disappear from my sight." I certainly did disappear. I ran. I took small backways, avoiding the main streets where the military patrols could stop me. Before reaching home, I found some of the neighbors assembled on the street, and they seemed astonished to see me coming back. It was from them that I discovered the truth.

"They have released you?" they asked as if they had not expected to see me again.

"But why should they take me? What have I done?" I answered in utter amazement.

"Oh, you are the only one not to know what has happened. Don't you know all the Tutsis are being rounded up because they have helped the *Inyenzi* who attacked the city last night?"

"Is that so? I didn't know," I told them and hastened to go home, just in case the soldiers came back. I did not want to be seen. My heart was troubled, and for the first time I felt deeply, terribly scared. *They are doing it again, like in 1963 when they rounded up our fathers, accusing them of supporting the Tutsis in exile. But I have not supported anybody. I did not even know that the RPF existed. Why should they take innocent people?* As I pondered all this in my heart, my former rage surged back with that feeling of hopelessness that comes with knowing there is nothing you can do against a system that will not even give you the chance to defend your innocence. Penina was overjoyed to see me back, but fear gripped her when I told her what I had learned during the short trip back.

That was Friday, and I decided to spend the Saturday in fasting and prayer to find the mind of the Lord. What should I do in such a situation? I came out of the day with a promise from the Lord that he would protect us through the situation. God told me not to engage in war or battle. "Pray and wait until this is over. Keep your heart clean of anger, hatred, and bitterness. Guard your heart; I will guard you." My meditation that day turned again on the cross, and I decided to keep my eyes fixed on Christ and to adopt a Christ-like position and attitude in every situation. I left the prayer room with peace in my heart and a firm determination not to allow whatever might happen to drag me back into ethnic hatred.

In the following days, we were to hear that many members of our two families had been rounded up; our parents had been forced to go into exile in Uganda. For four years we did not get any news of them. Our first daughter was born during this period, and it was painful to miss the family rejoicing that usually accompanies such occasions.

Walking the streets became a real nightmare, always being stopped by unfriendly soldiers and policemen (*gendarmes* as they were called), and then later on came the extremist Hutu militias supported by the government.

It became four years of daily uncertainty and danger. My work consisted of frequent visits to the different university groups; there were two campuses in Kigali, one campus in Butare in the southern part of the country, and four in the North, — home to the most vicious Hutu extremists. There were military roadblocks at close intervals along the northern road, as close as every twenty kilometers, and for a Tutsi to pass them was always a nightmare, close to a miracle. I have seen people beaten for no other reason than having a Tutsi identity card, and I have seen others taken out of the buses accused of spying for the RPF, often never coming back.

Traveling to the northern areas was always a test of faith, and I had to pray long before deciding to go. On more than one occasion I escaped death by only a hair's breadth. Once, as I was coming from Busogo Campus in Ruhengeri, one of the soldiers at the Musanze roadblock took my identity card, put it into his pocket, and went on checking the other passengers. My heart started drumming inside, and I could feel the sweat slowly running down the inside of my arm. I silently prayed and asked the Lord to give me his protection and wisdom when I should open my mouth. I strengthened myself inside and decided to play it cool, ignoring all the danger. Eventually, the soldier came back to my level and asked me to come out of the vehicle. "This man," he said loud enough for everybody around to hear, "is carrying hand grenades in that briefcase."

That was enough accusation to terrify any person, but I felt quiet inside and told him, "I will not come down. The accusation is false. I don't have any hand grenades."

"What then is the weapon you are carrying in your briefcase? There is no way an *Inyenzi* can be traveling in this place without a weapon," he said very affirmatively.

I decided to play his game, and I turned the whole thing into humor. "Sure, I have a weapon, but it is bigger than a hand grenade ... it is a bomb." Everybody in the minibus turned around to look at this enemy who had been traveling with them. Before they could say anything, I opened my briefcase very wide for everybody to see: a pair of trousers, a shirt, a towel, a Bible, and a hymn book were all that was in the briefcase. I slowly took out my Bible and told the soldier. "Look, this is the only weapon I carry with me, and I know how to use it. This is the only weapon I believe in. I preach love and brotherhood, and I wish you all well."

All the other soldiers who had come to see the "catch" went into hysterics, and even my tormentor broke into a loud laughter. "That is a bomb, man. Here, take your card and go, and don't shell our position. And remember to pray for us," he said, still laughing. We drove off and I sat in prayerful silence, thanking the Lord for the rescue.

That kind of experience taught me a great lesson: if you want to love your enemies, look behind the mask of hatred, cruelty, and violence they display on the outside, and you will always find a human face. Talk to that face and forget about the ugly side you see with the eyes and hear with the ears. This does not mean they will always be good to you, but at least it will help you to love them and feel pity for them. This became a frequent exercise while I traveled throughout the country. And I often prayed this prayer, which I still often pray today: "Lord, help me to see beyond the appearances and help me to hear beyond the words." Deep inside, even what appears to be an ugly, evil individual hides a fearful, confused human heart.

On another occasion, a soldier on the roadblock at Shyorongi on that same road took my identity card, looked intently at me, and then said, "You! Why is your identity card so dirty?"

I knew what he meant, but I decided again to play ignorant and innocently retorted, "I'm sorry; I had not noticed that that piece of paper had gone dirty. You see, perhaps one of the many soldiers at the previous roadblocks had dirty hands."

The man caught the quip and became more insulting. "That is not what I mean. I ask you, 'Why is your identity dirty?'"

"Oh, sir, I did not know that is what you meant. But even for that, I'm totally innocent. When God created me, he did not ask for my advice; maybe if he had I would have begged him to put me on the clean side. We choose our friends; God determines our families." Some passengers who overheard our conversation giggled.

The man was taken aback, as if he did not expect me to answer back. He then looked at me intently in the eye, and as if to save face he asked, "Are you a '*murokore*' (born-again Christian)?

"Oh yes," I replied lightheartedly, trying to create a certain atmosphere of camaraderie to diffuse the tension.

"That was a good sermon, hhhn?" he commented, handing me my identity card and waving the minibus off. Whew! Another narrow escape! I could recount story upon story like this.

Traveling around during that period improved my faith and my prayer life tremendously, but it was still very trying to love and accept those persecuting me. "Lord, how do you expect me to love these people? How do you expect me to forgive all those undeserved insults? How do I love people who never seem to become good?"

There are times when we lure ourselves into thinking that loving our enemies will transform them into friends. It may happen in the case of neighbors (and even with them it is not guaranteed), but it is a different story when it is a system. I'm sure those soldiers never comprehended that I had forgiven their behavior, and I never had occasion to repay their evil with good. In such cases, experience has taught me that you love your enemies just because it matures you as "a son of your heavenly Father, who causes his sun to rise on the evil and the good, and sends rain on the righteous and the unrighteous" (Matt. 5:45). It also keeps your heart at peace. People's emotions have this great power — they transform our hearts into their own image! Live next to a person who hates you, and you become like him. Sit next to a grumbler, and chances are you will start grumbling like him! But loving your enemy is not an emotion; it is a decision, a firm refusal to let the evil deeds of your enemy shape you into his ugly image. When our vulnerable and easily changing emotions would lead us steadily into destruction, love lifts us out of it. This may sound easy on paper, but it was a real cross to carry, and at times it was too heavy. I have to confess there were days when my old liberation dreams would come back stronger, and on many occasions I felt like joining the RPF in the bush. But this time I had a wife and a baby girl, and the Lord had expressly told me to keep out of the fight. How well he knew me!

My wife Penina was not as lucky in her workplace, where many tended towards extremism. She was at that time a secretary with the Water and Electricity Company, and she would come home every day with sad stories of negative insinuations, insults, and even assaults. Then one day they decided she was too much of a nuisance in the secretariat where all the customers passed by her, and they sent her to the water purification station, a long distance from home, just to make life impossible for her. Some weeks later, they again decided she was dangerous in that place because, they said, she would poison the water distribution system. The director of the station was a very reasonable person and defended her: "I can't imagine this young woman causing any threat to the city water system; you would need at least two lorries of deadly poison or a fast self-multiplying virus to create any threat to the city. Find more convincing evidence to fire her." The daily trauma of working in that kind of hate-filled environment became unbearable, and she eventually decided to resign from the company.

Meanwhile, the war had entered a ceasefire, and the RPF was negotiating with the Habyarimana administration for a transition government. The situation was complicated by the creation of different opposition political parties, and when we were not caught up in the fire of ethnic hatred, we were in the frying pan of political rivalries. The stated goal of the negotiations was to establish a set of protocols for power-sharing and peaceful implementation of laws guaranteeing a lasting peace. The Arusha Accords signed in August 1993 gave us hope that life was going back to normal, yet everything around us indicated otherwise. People were murdered every day, and the local Hutu militias were becoming more and more virulent and vicious. They were even seen training to kill. One evening a man was stabbed in the chest right in front of me, and I had to turn around running not to be seen by the murderers. It was out of the question to call for help — the power was in their hands and the authorities were on their side.

Another day I was attacked by a small group of young men and escaped with some bruises — fortunately the group did not use knives. I reported the case to the Deputy Officer of the Police in our area, who happened to be a brother in the Lord, and his answer was more than enlightening. "Look, Antoine, trust in God to keep you; do not put your hopes in us. Those *Interahamwe* (local militias) are protected by the government." He went on to tell me how he had captured and put under custody a group of *Interahamwe* who had knifed a man to death, and the following day orders had come from his superiors to release the "innocent young men you have unjustly locked up." Signing the Arusha Accords was not going to solve these problems. Every day the militia's mischievous behavior became more emboldened while they became better armed. Many houses were attacked with hand grenades, and many people were shot dead without reason. By the end of 1993 the situation had become unbearable.

One evening, while praying with some brothers, we decided to organize a week of preaching based on the theme "Get Reconciled to God and live at peace with one another." Israel Havugimana was the African Evangelistic Enterprise (AEE) Team Leader, and he was the initiator of the campaign that would cover the whole capital city, Kigali. Allow me to make a digression to introduce Israel. He was a Hutu but a born-again Christian who believed in reconciliation. He organized a Bible study prayer group in his home, and we always met Tuesday evenings. The group was mixed with Hutus and Tutsis, but we never considered those ethnic divisions; we were just brothers and sisters, carrying to the Lord all the fears and concerns of the nation. And it was from this weekly Bible study group that there emerged the idea of preaching to the nation a message of healing and reconciliation.

The City authorities gave us authorization to speak in different public places, churches, and stadiums, and the government allowed us to use the national radio station to broadcast the messages. But the militias in some places disturbed our meetings and prevented people from listening. On the evening of Friday, the 17th of December, I was preaching in the Gikondo area, and a group of *Interahamwe* militias came, picked up all the leaflets we had just finished distributing to the standing participants, tore them and burnt them into a heap of ashes. They prevented me from speaking, threatening us with stones and knives. I told the worship leaders to sing a song while I prayed for the Lord's guidance for a new message for the occasion. I felt boldness in my heart. I changed the message and preached on Habakkuk 2:12: "Woe to him who builds a city by bloodshed and establishes a town by crime!"

I was amazed to see how the militia kept quiet and listened to the prophetic message. At the end of the message, their leader came to me and said, "Why didn't you say it is the RPF that is killing people? You must be one of their accomplices."

I still felt fearless and boldly answered him: "I don't know who is doing it. If it is the RPF, then they are doomed; if it is you, then you too will face the judgment of God." The conversation went on for some time, and as we were finishing, I felt a strong urge to give him a warning message. I took the microphone and told all the gathering: "God is calling us to love each other. But all around it looks as if many people have chosen the path of violence. If as a nation we do not repent, by this time next year, not many of you will be here. Repent while it is still today."

It was during the closing rally of that same campaign that Israel Havugimana, who had pioneered the initiative, preached the message that many people still think cost him his life. He was powerfully outspoken, calling the leaders to their senses and telling everybody to repent of ethnic hatred, and the message was broadcast on national radio for the whole country to hear. That week was unquestionably prophetic and full of boldness. I still remember with awe how the Lord protected all of us during the deliveries.

By January 1994, the tension in the country in general and in Kigali city, in particular, had reached cataclysmic proportions. During the month of February, a contingent of 600 RPF soldiers came as escorts for their leaders, who were to be part of the transition Government in line with the Arusha Peace Agreement. They were stationed in the compound of the National Assembly Palace, a strategic place close to the Presidential Guards' camp, most probably to make their supervision easier. This brought some hope in the hearts of many, but it also created fear and tension among the Hutu extremists. Relatives, friends, and sympathizers who visited the RPF camp were secretly identified, followed and targeted for attacks. More people were dying every day, hand grenades were thrown into houses, and no authorities were doing anything about it. A hand grenade was lobbed into our friend Israel Havugimana's house, a few minutes after we had closed our Bible study meeting, and fortunately nobody was in the living room when it exploded. Later we learned that he had been betrayed by his watchman, who reported to the Security services that Israel was holding RPF meetings in his home under the pretense that it was a Bible study. Our Bible study meetings could have been easily confused for a political gathering because we often spoke openly about the details of the deteriorating political situation before turning the gathered information into prayer requests. It also happened that many of the Bible study group members were Tutsis, many of them having come to the Lord through our evangelistic outreach. In one significant meeting, we asked Israel to accept a pause of the Bible studies for a while so as not to jeopardize his life and his family.

"No!" he said, "what kind of testimony would that be if I denied my brothers at a time like this? What testimony would it be if I cowered in front of the threats of the evil I'm fighting against? The Lord will protect me, and if it is his will that I go, I will gladly die for what I believe in."

And he did die for what he believed in. On Tuesday, April 5, we had an overnight prayer time for the healing of the nation, and the Lord told us to mobilize the country for prayer using 2 Chronicles 7:13–14 where the Bible says: "when I shut up the heavens so there is no rain, or command locusts to devour the land or send a plague among my people, if my people who are called by my Name, will humble themselves and pray and seek my face and turn from their wicked ways, then I will hear from heaven and will forgive their sin and will heal their land." From these verses we wrote a flyer to send to the churches all over the land, and Israel took it to the printers the following day. But the devil had been faster! That same date, on the night of April 6, the plane of the President was shot and the genocide bomb was detonated. On April 7, the very first day of the mayhem, Israel was among the first people to be killed with everybody who was found in his house. Only his second daughter, Daniella, was rescued by a Belgian doctor who lived next to their compound. All the team who had prayed with us that night was killed during the genocide, Hutu and Tutsi alike, and I was the only one who survived, left to tell and to carry on our hopes.

Chapter Seven

THROUGH THE VALLEY
OF THE SHADOW OF DEATH

"Even when I walk in the valley of the shadow of death, I will fear no evil,
For you are with me; your rod and your staff, they comfort me"
Psalm 23:4

APRIL 7, 1994, 1:00 AM. We were awakened by the noise of gun shots coming from the hill in front of our house. I got out of bed, stood in the window, and watched as the sky grew red from the exchange of bullets.

"I guess this time war has broken out between the RPF contingent and the Republican Guards," I told my wife who was already panicking. Isolated sporadic gun shots could be heard from other cardinal points of Kigali, particularly in the eastern part of town, near Kanombe International Airport. We later learned that people were being gunned down by the presidential guards all over the city. We went back to bed, puzzled, not sure of what was happening. Was it war or just a short-lived confrontation?

The following day, I woke up early to get ready to go to a pastors' retreat in Shyogwe Anglican Diocese. The noise of gun shots had receded but sporadic firing could still be heard from some spots in the city. I switched the radio on to listen to the morning news, and the first sounds that came out were of a slow and mournful classical song. I waited before turning the radio off, thinking this was a musical interlude before the news. Then came the announcement, "The Ministry of Defense has the sorrow to announce to all the population that his Excellency's (the President of the Republic) plane has been shot down and that he has died along with all his company, among them the President of Burundi. Everyone is asked to stay home until further notice." I shuddered. "This is trouble," I told my wife before going out, just to see if the sun had risen as usual!

Our house helper Beatrice was already up, and she was sweeping the backyard with her younger sister Donata who had come to visit. Dinah, my wife's younger sister was washing the dishes in the kitchen, while Jeremiah, my wife's cousin, was in front of the house watching what was happening. I stood in the backyard and called our neighbor, trying to start a conversation. He was already up and was standing behind his house, smoking a cigarette. He looked quite agitated and nervous.

"Good morning," I greeted him. Silence answered. I repeated the greeting, thinking he had not heard me.

He grumbled back, "Haven't you heard what has happened?"

"Yes, I have," I answered back, not sure if it was the right thing to say, just waiting for more from him.

"Hmm, hmm," he cleared his throat and spat. "How could such a thing be avoided when the enemies are all around us," he said, making a circular gesture with his arm as if to represent being surrounded by enemies. And the gesture included my home — at least that is how I interpreted it.

"Do you know who did it?" I asked with some feigned innocence.

"Who needs to be told? It is the RPF and their Tutsi accomplices. And they are everywhere," he said affirmatively, without any further comments. He threw the cigarette butt on the ground, crushed it with his foot, and hurried back into the house. Some minutes later, he came out with a machete and left. I stood outside musing for a while before going back into our bedroom to report to my wife the short conversation with our neighbor. We sat on the bed, not knowing what to do next.

It was around 7:30am, and we decided it was best to pray, and to wait and see. Then all of a sudden Jeremiah called us to come out quickly and see. We ignored the call and went on with our prayers. His calling became more pressing. We shortened our intercession and went out. We stood in front of the house and looked at where he was pointing, at the Hotel Chez Lando a short distance from our home. People were running in all directions carrying things, hiding them, and going back for more. Then we saw smoke coming from the hotel. We thought they had set it on fire. Some minutes later, the sons of our neighbor came carrying some of the plunder, joyfully reporting on the death of some of the people in the area. It was through their comments that we learned that road blocks had been placed in all the streets and the *Interahamwe* were controlling all movements. We panicked, went into the living room and spontaneously started prayers, pleading with God for our own safety and the security of friends around the country. In the meantime, the noises grew louder and nearer, and we could hear from our neighbor's house the regular reports given by the young men about the different neighbors who had been killed.

Time went by very slowly, and we did not know what to expect. We stopped all our chores and simply sat in the house, not even talking to each other. Through the front windows we could see dust rising every time a shell hit the concrete wall of the Palace of the Parliament where the RPF contingent and their leaders were housed. We pitied them and wondered if any would survive. That was the only distraction we had, along with the regular reports of the young men to their sisters next door. Around 3:30pm we heard noises getting nearer to our home. Peninah was in the bedroom breastfeeding Deborah, our young daughter who was the only person who seemed to enjoy the loud noise of blasting shells. Beatrice and Donata were in the kitchen, while Jeremiah and Dinah were in another room where I had confined them because every time they looked out they tended to become more panicky. I looked through the window and saw a group of *Interahamwe* just outside the fence of our compound.

They were discussing whether to first throw a hand grenade into the compound or just to break in. "This is our turn," I told myself and immediately wild and weird thoughts whirled in my mind at a flashing speed. "Am I going to let them rape my wife, kill my child and all these young men in my home under my very eyes without even some attempt to protect them? What type of death are we going to die? Are they going to shoot us or cut us into pieces?" I shuddered. Then the idea crossed my mind: *Why don't you take a stick or some other weapon at hand and go out and fight them? Can't you die like a man?* This was my spontaneous, human reaction. I could recognize my old self surging up, like in the past; I could never have tolerated being ill-treated without some reaction. Old memories from school flashed back in my mind when we had stood face to face with other students, ready to fight our way out during the 1973 Tutsi massacres. Our resistance was rewarded then, but this time something was missing. I didn't have the inner conviction. And there was no peer support. And then

I remembered the promises the Lord had given us during our morning prayers: "He who dwells in the shelter of the Most High will rest in the shadow of the Almighty. I will say of the Lord, 'He is my refuge and my fortress, my God in whom I trust'" (Ps.91:1–2).

I remembered other words the Lord had given the previous week when I went to preach at a retreat, and then violence broke out when I was on the way. "Have mercy on me, O God, have mercy on me for in you my soul takes refuge. I will take refuge in the shadow of your wings until the disaster has passed" (Ps 57:1). In these instantaneous reflections, I felt my spirit growing calmer, and I heard a quiet voice inside, telling me, *You have been preaching sermons on loving and praying for your enemies, and now you want to die shedding blood. Instead of trying to "die like a man" why don't you just "die like a Christian?"* I was deeply convicted as I remembered all the past efforts I had made to keep my heart pure from anger and bitterness, and I made this short prayer of confession: "Lord, forgive me for thinking of taking up my own defense, and help me to obey you even unto death. Give me favor with these people, and if it is your will that we die, give me time to die praying for them as you did on the cross."

At that very moment, a feeling of deep peace that I had never experienced before came all over me, and I felt so light inside that a breeze could have swept me off the ground. I had expected to die and knew what I would do when the killers came. Nothing else mattered anymore. I was ready to face death like Christ and was anxious to experience the life awaiting me after death. I felt the reality of the hope set before me.

As soon as I made these realizations and sorted myself out, the staccato of a machine gun came from the street in front of our compound. "These are *Inyenzi!*" the *Interahamwe* said as they scattered at a run uphill. I did not have an opportunity to see those "liberators" and just sat where I was, pondering the incident. The experience took less than five minutes but seemed to span a lifetime. The following days were going to be filled with horrendous scenes, but this episode was like a vaccine against the traumatic events we were going to live through. The peace that had come upon me and that spirit of forgiveness stayed with me even when I heard of the death of relatives and of many close friends. It comforted me on the tiring road of flight and strengthened me through the hardships and scarcity of a displaced persons' camp.

We stayed home for a week until, on Sunday the 17th, we packed a few things and joined others at the National Amahoro Stadium. The place was under the protection of the Bangladeshi battalion of the UN forces (UNAMIR), but the area surrounding it was a no man's land, some areas being under the control of RPF soldiers and others still controlled by the government army and the militias. Day and night artillery exchanges and the different sounds of small and heavy machine guns had become part of our daily experience. By the time we got to the stadium, making our way swiftly and silently through deserted side streets, there was no space left in the few rooms that were there. My brother-in-law Ignace Mwizerwa and his family were already there, and we simply joined them under the stairs of Entry 6, at the far eastern side of the stadium. It was the rainy season and the nights were wet and damp. At night the adults would sleep on the outer sides of the stairs to serve as a protective wall for the younger children. As it was near our home, we had brought with us our blankets and even some thin mattresses and warm clothing. Life was already bad but the worst was still to come.

Early on the morning of Tuesday the 19th, the government Army started shelling our refuge. A mortar whistled past our stairs and exploded some three meters away; fortunately no shrapnel came our way. Everybody started shouting as another mortar fell in Stairway 8, another in Stairways 10 and 12, and another in the middle of the big crowd of women who were up early cooking porridge for the children. It was a general stampede, people running and falling upon each other, shouting and yelling. Once the shelling stopped and the panic died off, we started sorting through the wounded and dead. The Red Cross arrived, and we helped move the wounded. I don't think anybody tallied the wounded; the dead numbered thirty-five, if I remember correctly.

The whole incident lasted for less than two hours, but by the time we finished cleaning the camp, everybody was desperate. I looked for a corner out of the way to pray. I needed reassurance, comfort, and strength. My hands were thick with blood, and my heart was heavy with anger, brewing with revolt. I cried to the Lord, big tears streaming down my cheeks, "How long, Lord, how long will you see this without doing anything about it? How long will innocent people die at the hands of the wicked? Lord, do you really care?" I did not care about those who passed by and saw me; after all, everybody had become emotional, some weeping, others screaming; the whole camp was in tears and utter disarray. I vented all my anger in the presence of the Lord, and by the time my emotions were spent, I felt peaceful inside. The Lord softly reminded me of these words that were to come to me many times during my trials: *This is the time to uproot and to tear down, the time to destroy and to overthrow, then will come the time to build and to plant. I'm making everything new. So, "be still and know I am God."* I wiped my face with the sleeve of my shirt and went back to Stairway 6. The blood on my hands had now dried, but for many days I would rub my hands as if to get rid of the sticky sensation. The smell of fresh blood remained in my nostrils for I don't know how many weeks. The smell and touch of blood, the screams of the wounded and horrible sights of the dead torn into pieces can sear your mind like a hot iron, haunting you nightmarishly even during the day.

That day we all lost trust in the protection of the UNAMIR. The Bangladeshi soldiers had run behind their cover, and although they did come to help lift the dead and wounded, there was nothing else they could do to protect us. Their big guns were all there, pointing in the air, aiming at nothing, silent like big toys. Not even one mortar was shot to tell our killers that this was a protected zone. It was not part of their mandate. From the beginning of the killings, people had died in front of that camp and the soldiers on lookout positions had not even moved the few meters across the road to rescue those who were being massacred. This was not part of their mandate either. Instead their mandate was to be "Peacekeepers, not peacemakers." They were not here to protect us, just to observe how we died. The world had not only given us over to death, they had cynically deployed people and paid them to observe how we would die! It took me time to forgive that faceless body we call "the world." And then I came to my senses. After all, why blame the world for not coming to our protection when it was our own people killing us?

The stadium was a UNAMIR controlled area, but RPF soldiers disguised as civilians did come and go easily. That is how we were informed that those who wanted to leave and go to a safer place in the RPF controlled zone would be helped to go by night, but they did not tell us when that would be. We always went to bed very early and had been asked not to light any fire by night — because these would betray our positions to the militias and government soldiers. Although we went to bed early, we never slept deeply.

81

On Sunday the 24th, around 9p.m., just as we slipped under the blankets, we heard people moving from place to place murmuring, "Those who want to go, this is the time! Hurry." It was not too difficult for us to go since we had kept our few possessions packed in bags. We swiftly packed a few of the kitchen utensils we could get hold of in the dark and joined the crowd. There was a light drizzle, and the sky was covered with heavy black clouds threateningly pregnant with more rain. The night was pitch black, the ground muddy with puddles from the rain in many places. We did not know where we were going, but we trusted our guides knew. Around 5,000 people trekked out of Kigali that night, headed toward an unknown destination. Somewhere in the middle of the journey I lost touch with Penina and Beatrice, our house helper, who was carrying our daughter Deborah. I was worried the entire way. We had to move in total silence, literally on tiptoe, not making any noise to avoid the attention of the government soldiers.

Around 3a.m. we came to the paved road at Kabuye and were told to rest and camp until further notice. We were even allowed to talk again. The night had grown thick, and it continued to rain. My clothes were wet, my whole body shivering from the cold, and I worried about the whereabouts of my family. The distance we had covered was not so far, around 15 kilometers, but it had been exhausting to move without talking, stepping silently and through mud during the dark wet night. I went looking for a place to rest, having decided I would wait for daybreak to look for Penina and the others. I went to a pile of bricks I had stumbled on at the border of the road and found others had gotten there before me, including Penina and the whole family group. My heart warmed, and we were all happy to be reunited. But deep inside, my heart was still dampened, heavy, and gloomy.

I sat on the pile of bricks and said a short prayer of thanksgiving sprinkled with some despair. I remember I finished asking, "Lord, are you really in this? Are you really here?" Then this verse from Isaiah 43 came dancing in my mind, "When you pass through the waters, I will be with you; and when you pass through the rivers, they will not sweep over you. When you walk through the fire, you will not be burned; the flames will not set you ablaze. For I am the Lord your God." These words came as a soothing balm on my wearied soul, and I went to sleep! It was 6:30a.m. when I woke up (I still had my watch), and it was still drizzling.

Penina remarked, "I have seen you sleep in pretty difficult circumstances, but I could not imagine seeing you deep asleep in the open, sitting in the mud under the rain!"

"That's the peace the Lord gives to those who trust in Him," I told her jokingly. Through the short rest I had recovered my spirits, and I was even feeling more confident despite the hard situation. I knew the Lord was in control, and that was enough. It was now daytime; the rain finally stopped and everybody was wondering what was next.

Most of the young soldiers who had served as our guides left and only a few stayed with us to protect the camp. Eventually orders came, "Everybody find a place to stay; all the houses around here are empty." There was a real scramble for accommodation. Kabuye is a small satellite town outside Kigali city, and there were at least three government projects in the area. The residences and the offices of those projects became our transit camp. I was standing in front of a house when the information got to me, and it did not take me long to break the door with an axe I had seen in the kitchen in the back. Once well settled inside, the next challenge was to find water and food. By midday, some of the young soldiers who had been left behind to protect the camp started taunting us, "No wonder they kill you like rabbits! You have not been taught to fight for your lives! We hope you are not waiting for us to go into the fields to pick up vegetables and cook food for you! Get out into the fields and find food for your families."

Nearby was a government project farm with ducks, rabbits, chickens, and pigs; the whole valley was ripe with beans and potatoes. In the twinkling of an eye all the birds, rabbits, and pigs were dead and the camp became like a beehive of people fetching food. Firewood was not a problem but clean water proved to be scarce. The water in the valley was full of decaying corpses, and wherever we turned there was no fresh water to be found. I remember standing near the house, an empty jerrican in my hands after an unsuccessful hunt for water, and I cried to the Lord, "If you are here, Lord, where is the water?" No sooner had I finished my prayer than somebody passed by with a saucepan full of water. A large water tank had been found in one of the compounds and people were scrambling for it. Not many had the presence of mind to come with containers, so I found the queue not very long and managed to get our share of water. I knew water would soon be a problem but at least for that day we were well provided for. After all, we did not even know when we would break camp again; having been told it would be "soon" but nothing else. So we were on standby with plenty of food in the surrounding fields but with little water.

Living with this kind of uncertainty for tomorrow's provision was going to become our lifestyle for the days to come. It is difficult and trying to live one day at a time, thankful for today and not worrying about tomorrow! Anyone who has never lived this way cannot imagine how traumatic it can be. On the other hand, there is no better training for one's faith. When your bank account, your life, and medical insurance are no longer your source of security, when your national army and your national police have failed you, when your money has turned into paper pulp in your pocket and the few banknotes that survived cannot buy anything because there is no store around you, then you understand what it really means to live by faith. In the quiet of the evening, I looked past the smoke-covered valley to the low hills cloaked in mist, and my mind turned thankfully to these words of Psalm 121: "I lift up my eyes to the hills, where does my help come from? My help comes from the Lord, the Maker of heaven and earth." This comforted my heart.

Our stay in Kabuye was brief; by Tuesday the first group was transported to Byumba, a town near our northern border with Uganda. We were told that they waited for the fighting to settle down in that corridor, as government soldiers fleeing from the advance of the RPF had just crossed the road a few kilometers north of the place we were camped. This time we did not travel together; the women with children were given priority, and they left on big lorries the RPF soldiers had taken from the Kabuye sugar factory and other places. For two days, five large lorries carried the people from morning until evening. All the baggage had been left behind, and every family left one or two people to look after their few possessions. I was among those scheduled to leave last, but suddenly the transport system broke down. The lorries were needed to transport weapons to the frontline, and we were asked to walk. My heart sank. It was already 1p.m., and there was no chance we would make it to Byumba before nightfall. But it was an order. We had to vacate the premises because they already installed heavy artillery on top of one of the hills and were already shelling Kigali. Our position would be under attack any moment.

Our group was not large, numbering around one thousand. We had a total of six soldiers to escort us. I pitied the young soldiers who were assigned the task because they just came back from the front to rest. Two went ahead, three dispersed in the middle rows, and one was left behind to close the rear. I decided to walk in the back rows to avoid the pressure of having to set pace in the front rows, and one of the soldiers marched beside us. You could tell he was in a bad mood, tired and hungry. At one place a gang of militia rushed toward us from the top of the hill throwing stones and brandishing their machetes and clubs with loud shouts, not having seen the soldiers. People started closing in together in fear. I kept looking at the young soldier, expecting him to do something, but all he did was move inside the row as if to hide among the crowd as the raging mob was closing in. I was scared because I was on the outer row, and I kept my eyes on the young soldier.

He discreetly cocked his gun and started moving toward the back and then all of a sudden, when the attacking mob was getting almost on us he started shooting at close range. He kept firing, and in less than five minutes the gang had dispersed, but many had been killed and wounded. The young soldier mumbled to himself, "Band of murderers, when will they understand everybody needs to live? And to think our *Afandis* (the officers) tell us not to shoot them!"

I looked at the boy, and my heart went out to him. I started thinking, *Maybe he too has lost his family and is dreaming of a time when he will be able to live without any threat on his life.* The following minute my heart was musing at how hard it will be to keep these young men from shooting the murderous mobs they would find on their way. That day I decided to pray for protection for the people and for the patience of the soldiers. How do you keep your cool when you find your father, mother, brothers, and sisters all dead, and you know the murderers are among those people you see in front of you? How could you possibly hold your anger? This was going to be a time of testing for their discipline. We marched on, the sun beating down upon us. We were exhausted; finally, by 4 p.m. we saw the lorries come from behind, and we were relieved.

Penina had found a place in Byumba in one of the classrooms of the Byumba Primary School — where about forty other people were already staying. We slept there for several days, then joined two other families who were staying in a small two-roomed house on their own. Twenty-three of us stayed together in that small place, but it was more intimate because we did not have to share things with strangers. The place had a kitchen, an outdoor pit-toilet, and a room we used as a bathroom, but there was no running water. Every day we had to go down the steep hill and fetch water from a well in the valley.

By the end of April, the camp had grown to around 10,000 people, and it kept increasing until we left in July, when the people numbered around 20,000. There were medical facilities, but the hospital was always overcrowded. The RPF was in charge of the camp, and they had assigned teams to look after all our needs. They really went to great lengths to make our stay as livable as it could be. Once settled, many relief organizations started flocking in: The International Committee of the Red Cross, the World Food Program, World Vision International, Compassion International, and many other international this or that. They all came with their specialized responses to different needs in the camp — food, blankets, saucepans, plates, cups, and medicine. Dried corn, lentils, and beans were our staple foods from Monday to Sunday. Corn for lunch, corn for supper, corn for the entire week. The only way to afford variety was to use your own money and buy rice or other food items, but not many people had money. We had all left in a rush, and there were no banks in the displaced persons' camps. Those who had friends or relatives in Uganda could ask for travel permits to visit them, but again, movement was very limited in the camp to curtail chaos and disorder. We slowly grew accustomed to the hardships of camp life. The most annoying thing was the idleness, waking up in the morning and doing nothing for the whole day.

People spent the day in groups gathered around radios, listening and commenting on the recent news, switching channels to get different versions of the same news, hoping for some good information about the progress of the war. Everybody was interested to hear what was going on in the war zone, and every day we were jubilant to hear that the RPF was advancing and occupying more territory. Whenever we wanted to get an inside view of the battle, we would switch on the RTLM (Radio Television Libre des Mille Collines), the radio of the Hutu extremists. From morning until evening, it was unceasingly spewing out its hate-filled propaganda, but it also gave us good insights into the fears on the other side and how far they had run. At times they even gave names of people who had been found and killed or were being hunted.

Our other source of news came from the new arrivals, people who were rescued in different parts of the country and were brought to Byumba. Everybody was interested to know if friends and relatives were still alive, but most of the time the news that came was disheartening. I remember the day one of our friends came into the camp during the month of June. We all flocked around him to learn of our prayer group, but the news was all depressing. Israel Havugimana, dead with his father and all the family. Charles and Phoebe, dead. Rukaka and Beata, dead with all the family. Speciose, dead. Simon Pierre Mugabo, dead, but Jacqueline has survived with the children. Nepo and Jeanne Rose? Dead... Simon Pierre Mugabo had been my best man at our wedding, and I had been Nepo's best man. These were very close friends. And they were all dead. He went on telling us the details of how each was killed, how he got the news, and so on. And that was the same story in every group you passed or joined. Every day came with the bad news of friends, colleagues, and relatives who had been massacred.

But life was still going on. I was amazed to see how people took all the sad news as normal. I think we were all still numb from our recent experiences. How could we ever recover? When you have seen so many people dying around you, and you get to the point it becomes normal, something in you dies and does not easily come back. All the way up to Byumba, dead bodies were part of the landscape; we passed them, sat near them, jumped over them, and stumbled on them in the dark of the night. Finally, we had lost the sense of horror at the sight of a corpse, and we listened to the sad news of parents, brothers, sisters, and friends who had been cruelly murdered, and it seemed not to affect us. We had grown insensitive, our hearts numbed. We had lived through and seen too much to be affected or to care anymore.

As days went by and life in the camp moved from crisis to routine, people started to long for the comforts they had left behind, and our sense of community began to erode. Relationships became tense, fighting began, and those who lived together got more and more selfish as some of the ordinary commodities like salt, sugar, soap, and toothpaste became luxuries. Sexual promiscuity was becoming the standard.

Our three families stayed together, in harmony, and we were lucky enough to have escaped with some money. Around the middle of May, the International Fellowship of Evangelical Students, for whom I worked in campus ministry, had learned of my whereabouts and sent me 300 dollars, a colossal sum in the camp. I decided not to succumb to the selfish spirit of the time, and after exchanging the money for Ugandan shillings, I bought a large carton of soap and put it at the disposal of all of us to use. Wherever I heard a brother or a sister complaining about this or that, I would use the money and provide. Penina was two months pregnant when we left Kigali, and the whole time in the camp was a real Calvary for her. She was always sick in the morning, and her stomach was not able to tolerate the corn. The simple smell of things made her vomit. I always felt pity for her but felt guilty at my powerlessness to do anything. The place was so congested that it was not even possible to get time or a place to ourselves so that we could share what we were going through. The money came as a godsend and allowed us some variety in our diet.

I began working with World Vision, helping with the distribution of relief amenities for the newcomers in Byumba and later on with another camp that had been started in Rutare, some 30 kilometers away. This was seen as our duty, and the RPF asked all the NGOs using Rwandese not to pay us. Everybody, they said, should work for the people, not for money, and since there were not enough jobs for all, the best way to avoid jealousy was to make us serve without getting paid. This policy paid off: not many people rushed to serve, only those who had the heart for it.

With an eye to justice along with compassion, one NGO gave workers food and other small remunerations like soap, sugar, and toothpaste, but nothing more. I worked in the World Vision aid distribution during the mornings and was always busy with the Christian Committee organizing Christian meetings and Bible study groups in the afternoons — a great opportunity to encourage the brothers and sisters through the Word. I had left with my small leather bag carrying a Bible, a hymn book, and a note-book. That bag was always strapped around my neck, as I was determined that if I were to lose everything else, I should not lose my Bible. That bag served as a pillow when we were sleeping, and I often used it as a sitting cushion when we had to sit in the dust or mud. Reading from the Bible and praying were my constant sources of comfort when my heart felt low.

IFES had not only sent me money, they later sent Richard Nuwaman-ya from FOCUS Uganda to inquire if I would be interested in leaving the camp for study while waiting for the situation in Rwanda to become clear. Nobody at that time could see how the whole thing would end, as the whole world thought Rwanda was going to become another Somalia. I rejoiced at the offer, and Richard went back to Uganda promising to come back soon. I spent time praising God for remembering me in my dire situation, but when I prayed about the issue of leaving the camp, I clearly sensed the Lord telling me not to go anywhere. *Stay with your people, suffer with them, serve them, and when the time comes, you will rejoice with them. If you leave Rwanda now, you will have no ministry when things are well settled.* It has never been difficult for me to obey when the voice of the Lord is clear. I prayed and waited for Richard to come back. He came with a letter of encouragement from Zac Niringiye who was then General Secretary of IFES for English-Speaking Africa. On a small piece of paper he had scribbled in quick handwriting, "We were glad to hear you are still alive. Be strong in the Lord and serve him faithfully." And he had added these verses from 2 Corinthians 1:3–4: "Praise be to the God and Father of our Lord Jesus-Christ, the Father of compassion and the God of all comfort, who comforts us in all our troubles, so that we can comfort those in any trouble with the comfort we ourselves have received from God." Then he had added, "I feel the Lord wants you to be his instrument in healing your nation." I'm sure he could not imagine that this message was a confirmation that the Lord wanted me to stay in Rwanda and 2 Corinthians 1:3–4 would be, two months later, the passage the Lord used to define my ministry in the country. I gave Richard my answer and asked him to send it to IFES with my gratitude. We prayed together, and he went back to Uganda.

By July the fighting had moved to the Northwest and the good news came — Kigali city had fallen into the hands of the RPF on July 4th. Everybody started dreaming of going back home, and with the dreams came trauma. All of a sudden, the reality dawned on many that they had no one and nothing to go back to. Many had lost their families, many children had lost both parents, husbands had lost track of their wives and children. News had been coming to us that many houses had been destroyed, that all the homes had been broken into and the possessions looted. What had been indifferent to us in the past became a haunting reality when we were told we would soon be free to go home. Go back, yes, but where? To join whom? To do what? The morale in the camp dropped very low. Even those of us who had our families with us did not dare rejoice openly when we knew many were going back to live in solitude. Comforting the weeping widows and orphans became our daily activity while waiting for the day to leave the displaced persons' camp.

Chapter Eight

SPEAKING INTO THE VALLEY OF DRY BONES

"All this is from God, who reconciled us to Himself
and gave us the ministry of reconciliation"
2 Corinthians 5:18

ONE MORNING IN JULY while everybody was impatiently waiting for
the green light to leave the displaced persons' camp, I sat in my usual place
behind the house to pray, asking God what exactly I should be doing in
the future. I knew the Lord had clearly told me not to serve in politics, although many of my friends were trying to convince me to join in the civil
service. It was true the country needed every educated person available
since most of the qualified people were either dead or had left the country;
the problem of competent manpower was crucial. But I knew the Lord
wanted me somewhere else; the question was where. I took a day off to
pray and find guidance. The verse Zac Niringiye had sent me and his comment came back in full light: "Comfort others with the comfort you have
received from God," and "be an instrument in the healing of the nation." I
had a clear mission statement for life. That morning I left the place hum-
ming the tune of a new song, and the words kept coming. In the evening I
took a notebook and wrote them down.

Refrain:
Sanga Umwami Yesu agukize agahinda,
Go to the Lord Jesus and let him heal your sadness
Jya umubwira byose azajya akuruhura,
Tell him all and he will give you rest
Aragukunda, aragushaka kandi umva ubu ari ho arakomanga (x2).
He loves you, he is seeking you, and he is knocking at your life's door.

Ufite abantu bakomerekeje umutima wawe,
You have many who have wounded your heart
Wagerageje kubababarira birakunanira,
You have tried to forgive but find you cannot
Egera Yesu ubimubwire n'urwango narwo araruruhura.
Get closer to Jesus, and tell him all, for he gives rest even from hatred.

Wanyuze mu ntambara zakomerekeje umutima wawe
You have passed troubles that have wounded your heart
Wibuka ibyo wabonye ishavu rikakubuza gusinzira
Remembering trials brings sleep-stealing sorrow
Egera Yesu ubimubwire n'ishavu naryo arariruhura.
Get closer to Jesus, and tell him all, for he gives healing even from sadness.

Wibaza ibibazo byinshi mu buzima bwawe
You have many worries about your life
Utekereza uko ejo uzamera bikakubera urujijo
When you consider tomorrow, you see only darkness
Egera Yesu ubimubwire n'ejonzamerante arayiruhura
Get closer to Jesus, and tell him all, for he heals even worries about what tomorrow will be.

I have often sung that song after preaching on healing and forgiveness, and I have seen people deeply touched, coming for prayer with tears streaming down their cheeks, giving over to the Lord the burden of their inner wounds, hatred, and bitterness.

91

On July 17th, I boarded a vehicle going to Kigali in order to explore the situation before taking my family back. I needed to be sure we would have a place to go back to, and my heart was pounding with uncertainty and apprehension as I approached our neighborhood. Before we fled, I had had a premonition that houses would be broken into and looted, so we had left all the doors open so that anyone who wanted to take things would not have to damage the doors. When I arrived, I found the house was there, standing, and even most of the essential things were still there: the beds, the chairs, the tables, the fridge... only the shoes and clothes and some other small things had been taken. We later discovered that an RPF soldier who knew us had gone inside the house and recognized our pictures — he then put the house under protection. Since he had not seen our corpses in the house or in the compound, he guessed we were alive and in hiding somewhere.

I took the opportunity to visit the place where my sister Speciose and her husband Bosco used to live with their four children. Total desolation. The house had been razed to the ground; there was not a trace that this used to be a family compound. Somebody had turned the compound into a field and planted sweet potatoes in it. I left with tears in my eyes, my heart full of sadness, just trying to guess the kind of death they had died. I went back to Byumba and brought the family home.

Life was not very easy, but as this was common to all, it cushioned the blunt force of everything. Human nature tends to bear misfortune better when everybody else is in the same miserable condition. We came back with some basic survival goods, so the major challenge was to find food.

Very soon more people started joining our home. Astoundingly, we found that my sister Speciose, her husband Bosco, and their 2-year-old boy had miraculously survived, hidden in a neighbor's ceiling. The old man that hid them had heard a militia leader putting a price on their heads. So he hid them in the ceiling of his house. I was amazed and overjoyed when they came and joined us. Next to arrive were Yvonne and Diana, nieces to my wife and now orphans. Their parents had been massacred with their elder sister Jane. Yvonne had been given a heavy blow with a metal bar on her head and was left for dead, but she later recovered. Diana was 3 years old, and the murderers had left her among the corpses saying, "Don't kill this one, let her die of hunger and cold." They had destroyed the house, and she was left sitting next to the corpses of her parents and sisters in the cold of a morning drizzle. When Yvonne recovered her senses, she dragged herself and took the younger sister with her and fled, finally ending up in an orphanage run by Antoine Vater, a French philanthropist who refused to leave the children of Rwanda behind. His book *Je n'ai pas Pu Les Sauver Tous (I Couldn't Save Them All)* is a moving testimony of courage, dedication, and miracles.

Then came Dativa, the daughter of one of my cousins. All her family had been massacred, and she walked from village to village, ending up in Kigali. Then Rene came, a young man I had known in the Student Christian Union at the University. He was psychologically at a very low ebb, having lost his family and suffering the trauma of seeing people killed beside him every day. His plea was very poignant when he told me, "I need a place where I can live without having to think about tomorrow, a place where I will be able to eat without having to work." He joined the ranks. Others, too, joined us for short stays, others for longer periods. All the rooms were full; sometimes we used the living room, turning it into a sleeping place for new arrivals. One day one of the children commented, "If there comes one extra person, we will have to use the bathroom; it is the only vacant room left in this house." Our home became a mixed orphanage of old and young, and it was a great joy to see all those people there, eating and rejoicing in the little we had.

The joy came with some frustrations, too. Lack of privacy, overcrowding, and having to share everything wore on us. Managing the frequent shifts of moods and reconciling the different temperaments for harmonious living was another great challenge. Coming home after long hours of work to find this chaotic family atmosphere was another psychological exercise.

"There is nowhere to run away from the problems of this nation," I often told Penina my wife. "You kick them out of your office and find them nestled in your home." This kind of life changes you for better or worse. When life squeezes you from all sides, your real self comes out! Many families began this period with children in their homes, but when the stresses came, they sent them away; the sacrifice was too much and the price too high. As I was often away from home, Penina had to shoulder the psychological weight of the situation, and I could see it was taking a heavy toll on her. Her maternal instinct had to be shared among so many people, and some of them were not lovable at all. During that time our second daughter was born, and we called her "Jovanis Uwirinze," Jovanis (for Jehovah) to remind ourselves that the Lord is our banner of protection and "Uwirinze"— "Protected by God"— to remind us that the Lord had been faithful to the promises he had given to us through Psalm 91: "He who dwells in the shelter of the Most High will rest in the shadow of the Almighty."

When I look back, years after, I can say with the psalmist that "he who sows in tears will reap with rejoicing" (Ps. 126:5). I always rejoice when I see the fruit of those lives — those adults and children who went through our home now well-settled. Some are still with us, and they are a great pleasure to watch. It gives a sense of having contributed to someone's life. Through our sacrifice, they were given a chance, and through our poverty, they were made happy. Such joy in joining the Lord's work is more gratifying than the small delicacies we would have enjoyed had they not been there. Some people used to warn me and my wife that we should send some of the people away in order to create more room for ourselves; their concern was that our family relationships would deteriorate if we kept them all.

"You see," they often told my wife, "you will not be able to cook for your husband the good meals he loves, then he may feel neglected and will start looking for care somewhere else. . . ." I'm glad my wife never paid them any mind. Life is what you make of it, and things like joy, intimacy, and comfort can easily be redefined. What destroys family life is not so much the lack of privacy; it is the lack of common values. It is the absence of common goals. In actual fact, we grew closer to each other during those difficult days because we had to support and encourage each other to bear with the burdens of our mutual responsibilities. And we grew closer to the children because many of them needed a lot of love and attention to get them out of the abyss of depression and hopelessness.

Finding a job had not been a problem. For the first two weeks, I worked with World Vision International in the establishment of their Kigali office, but still I knew this was not my place. It was during this period that Berhanu Deresse, who was then Regional Coordinator of African Evangelistic Enterprise, Eastern Africa Region, came asking me to join AEE. The Lord has his own sense of humor! While all the other organizations that wanted to hire me were promising a good salary and other advantages, Berhanu's final comment was "you will have to put in a lot of faith. At this moment AEE is going through a financial crisis, and I don't promise money will come easily. But we will try our best to help." That same day we sat with some of the surviving board members and drafted an orientation for the work to be done, and the following day I went into the office to start work. Israel Havugimana, the Team Leader, was dead. Alphonse Karemangingo, the Project Coordinator, was dead with Julienne his wife. Joselyne the accountant was dead. Malachie Munyaneza, the head of the Evangelism Department, had not come back yet. Phoebe Nyiraneza, the Project Assistant, had gone to studies in the US. There was no reference, no one to show me around. I went into the office and started putting together the scattered papers, wondering where to begin. Everything valuable had been looted except tables and some chairs. I knelt down in the midst of the scattered papers and prayed a short prayer: "Lord, what is it that you have called me into? Show me the way through this." Everything around me was depressing.

The city was like a shadow of itself. There was no transport, water was irregular, electricity was back in only a few neighborhoods, the banks were not functioning, and people were either dead or nowhere to be seen. More than 500,000 children were estimated to be without parents, either because the parents were dead or had been separated from the children when they were fleeing. More than 3,000,000 people were still in the camps in Tanzania, in Burundi, and in the Congo, and some people were already talking about the possibility of war resuming very soon. In the meantime, a large number of rightly or falsely accused people were being caught and put in jail for their participation in the genocide, and the judicial system had totally crumbled. Revenge was taking place in some places, although the government was trying its best to curb it by punishing those who were caught taking the law into their own hands. Former exiles of the 50s, 60s, and 70s came back and occupied houses that did not belong to them, while the real owners were trying to get their homes back. Landmines and unexploded mortars were everywhere, corpses were still unburied, and occasionally one might enter an unoccupied house to find the decaying bodies of a whole family. The evening was the time when people met to try to figure out who was dead or still alive and where they were. It would have been very easy to get discouraged and just give up. And there I was, sitting in an empty office alone, wondering where to start. It is easy to give birth to children, but only God can resurrect the dead! Rebuilding this nation was like raising the dead from a tomb!

But the Lord had said, "Comfort the people with the comfort you have received from the Lord." Very soon we started working with widows and orphans, distributing food items and other domestic utensils to those who had come back. We started visiting the churches and encouraging them, for there were many very depressed because of what had happened. Many church leaders had left the country, and those who were present felt timid because of the heavy accusations against the church during the genocide.

Time went fast, and things began getting clearer. By 1995 AEE-Rwanda ministry had become well established. We toured the country, encouraging and strengthening church leaders to pick up the pieces and carry on. By February that year, we started our reconciliation program on the national radio. To preach healing, forgiveness, repentance, confession, and reconciliation was not easy at a time when everybody was angry and bitter. Even some people in government circles thought it was crazy to talk of reconciliation. The official line was justice, and the slogan was "fight against impunity." But we stubbornly pushed for reconciliation. Dr. Rhiannon Lloyd, a Christian psychiatrist from Wales, joined our team and started a wonderful ministry with church leaders, organizing seminars in different corners of the country.

We organized prayer rallies interceding for the healing and reconciliation of the Rwandan population. We preached reconciliation in small gatherings, on the radio, in stadium meetings, and whenever the opportunity came. Through this time, I began to understand the dynamics of preaching the message of the cross of Jesus for reconciliation. I often preached on sin and our alienation from God, and on God's response through the cross of Jesus — who took our sins and our iniquities so that we can be forgiven when we repent. To the survivors of the genocide we preached the cross, presenting Jesus who carried our pains and our sorrows so that we can heal and be able to forgive as he forgave those who crucified him. To those who had problems accepting themselves because of what they had done and had been rejected by their families, we told them about the great value God gave to us when Jesus died on the cross, redeeming us with his own blood. And I always substantiated these messages with testimonies from my personal life. Rhiannon Lloyd and the healing team traveled with a wooden cross where people would nail pieces of paper upon which they had written all their pains. And the release at the end of the exercise brought a powerful breath of peace.

Wherever we went, the harvest was always great because people were tender and responsive. I remember one day preaching in Kigali prison and talking about the blood of Jesus that washes our sins. One of the prisoners gradually grew fidgety in his seat, and by the time I had finished preaching, he stood up and asked one question, "Do you mean to tell us that the blood of Jesus washes all of our sins?" stressing the word "all."

I replied, "Yes, it washes *all* our sins."

The man was still standing and then he said, "Then let me confess what I have done." He confessed to the many people he had killed and all the cruelties he had committed. By the time he finished, he said, "For all this time since I did that, I have never been able to sleep. I always see the faces of those people. They come back to haunt my nights. I hate myself, and many times I have wished I was dead. But today for the first time I feel peace. Let them do with me what they want, but I have found peace in my heart just by confessing this."

After he sat down, for four full hours people stood up to confess one after the other. This was soon to become a regular phenomenon. In one prison, a week after a preaching visit, more than half the inmates freely confessed what they had done. The Spirit of the Lord was moving and is still moving mightily in the prisons. Even at this moment, the largest churches in Rwanda are inside the prisons!

In 2003, more than 19,000 prisoners who confessed their crimes were released from prison by a Presidential decree. Visiting one of the solidarity camps where the released prisoners were being prepared for social reintegration, I was surprised by one of the participants I did not know. He came hugging me as if I had been a long-lost friend or a brother and then said, "You don't know me, but may God bless you for your preaching. I heard one of your sermons, and it led me to confession, and here I am out of the prison because of that."

His words brought tears to my eyes! If he had known how hard it had been for me to make the decision to start preaching to them! If he knew how difficult it had been to explain why we were preaching to "those murderers who had killed our people!" I always remember the day when one genocide survivor came to me and said, "What you are doing is betrayal. How dare you preach to those murderers? Let them at least die in sin and go to hell; that is where they will get the right punishment for what they did to us! What if you preach to them and they repent and go to heaven after all they did to our people?" And here they were, thanking me as a benefactor! Such moments lifted my spirits, and I felt that all those pains, all those nights of prayer, all those weeks away from my family had not been in vain. The Lord is being glorified and people are being liberated not only in the heart but also in body. "Those who sow in tears will reap with joy."

The story that was to comfort my heart most came from an unexpected corner. One bright morning, I was going out to a meeting when in the corridor of the office I met a young lady who told me she wanted to see me urgently. I was in a rush, and in such situations I often fail to stop and listen. "I'm sorry," I told her, "I'm late for a meeting, but if you have a problem of school fees or any other matter that needs urgent intervention from AEE, you can see the project coordinator. This is an important meeting, and I don't want to be late." In my hurry, I had simply mistaken her for an orphan or a young widow looking for help, as that was the kind of visit I usually received during those hours.

Then she broke into tears and unexpectedly shouted aloud, "My name is Immaculee, I'm the daughter of Gashugi, and I want to talk to you! I want to apologize to you for what my father did. I want you to pray for me!"

That took me by surprise. I immediately changed all my plans for the day. Here was the daughter of the man who had rounded up our fathers at my home village of Ntete and taken them to their death; here was a golden opportunity for reconciliation. I took her to my office and sat her in a chair, and we started talking. I had decided this was a more important meeting not to miss.

Between her sobs, she started telling me her story: "I came to the meeting where you were preaching last week, and I heard you recounting how you have forgiven those who wronged you from childhood. That warmed my heart and encouraged me to see you. I have already committed my life to the Lord, but I still carry a heavy burden in my heart. From childhood I have been rejected and persecuted because of what my father did. In school other children mocked me and shunned me because they called me the daughter of a murderer. Then when the genocide and the war were over, many people came back from Uganda, and it became worse. Every time I make friends with people, later on when they discover who I am, they change their attitudes and shun my company. That has deeply wounded my heart. When I heard you talking about forgiving the enemies and telling where you are from, I immediately guessed that you, too, had been wounded by what my father did. I don't know if your father is among those who were killed by my father, but I just need somebody who has been hurt by what my father did. I want somebody to whom I can express my sincere apologies and ask for forgiveness on behalf of our family. That time when people started repenting on behalf of their groups, I had wanted to come to you, but I knew we would not have enough time to talk, so I decided to come and see you. Will you forgive us for what my father did, and would you please lay your hands on me and pray a blessing upon my life? I need to be released from the curse of what my father did."

I did not know what to do, but deep inside I was very happy. I called some team members into my office, and I recounted to them what had happened. I told them who the young lady was and told them I needed their presence as witnesses to the reality of what the cross of Jesus can do to reconcile people.

In their presence I declared, "Here is the daughter of the man I have always blamed for the death of my father, and she has come to ask for my forgiveness on behalf of her family. On behalf of my family and all the other families that have suffered from the hands of her father, I want to extend the hand of brotherhood to her and tell her that I have forgiven her. And I will not just lay hands on her; I want to hug her as we do in our culture when we meet after many days of absence. I have found a sister."

Tears had started streaming down my face, and Immaculee was still sobbing as she had been while recounting her story. I hugged her and started speaking forgiveness and blessings into her life and her family. One of the team members made a short prayer praising the Lord. This will remain a significant and memorable event in my life. I had always talked of loving your enemies, but here I had a real person to love and cherish — the daughter of the man who killed my father.

Since then we have been meeting on different occasions for counseling and comfort, as she is still facing many problems. Not everybody has forgiven her for what her father did. "The father has sinned and is no more, and the children bear the punishment" (Lam. 5:7). Here is a beautiful young lady, innocent from all cruelty and malice but suffering because of what her father did. I wish all had an understanding heart. I pray everyone could have a forgiving heart to give hope and a future to the younger generation like Immaculee. Imagine how many children, how many wives, parents, and relatives have suffered the shame of being related to a genocide perpetrator! The survivors of the genocide need healing but so do the perpetrators and their families. Crime is a double-edged sword; it wounds the victim but also the offender. I have heard many prisoners confessing the heavy weight of guilt they have been carrying in their hearts, which tells me the healing process will take a long time for this nation.

In one of the prisons, one man became mad and was always shouting, "Look at that child, why is she coming toward me, why is she smiling?" He repeated it often, and those who knew him say he killed the child of a neighbor who came to him smiling, thinking she had found refuge in the arms of family friend. That smile of an innocent 3-year-old child never left his mind, and the guilt of his deed drove him crazy. Another man was caught carrying a bag with human bones, and he explained, "I killed this man. He was a neighbor. He was a friend. I buried him, and one night his ghost came back and told me to go and unbury the bones and carry them wherever I go. And the day I will put them down, I will die." Here was another man, seared in his conscience by his crime. Now imagine the guilt of women forced to throw their children into rivers, husbands ordered to kill their own wives and children, friends who had to betray friends for survival.

The way home will be long, but we will walk the road and get there. He who has enabled us to get here will take us further. "Not by power nor by might but by my Spirit," says the Lord. Today we have heard thousands of stories of healing and forgiveness, stories of repentance and confession around the cross of Jesus Christ, and we have the firm confidence that reconciliation can be achieved to become a lifestyle.

Chapter Nine

PUBLICLY POLITICAL

"Blessed are the peacemakers, for they will be called sons of God"
Matthew 5:9

ONE MORNING in June or July of 1999, I received a call that sounded a bit strange to my ears. The caller introduced herself not by name but by a strange word! "This is the OTP, we would like to inform you that you have been chosen to be one of the commissioners on the National Unity and Reconciliation Commission to be announced in the coming days." OTP, National Unity and Reconciliation Commission? I paused a moment just to figure out what these titles meant, then I spoke back, "Who is OTP?"

The lady on the other end laughed but answered politely, "OTP is not a person; it is short for the Office of the President."

"Ah, ok," I answered — flattered to be called by the OTP! — "it will be a great pleasure and privilege for me to be on that commission, but let me tell you that I'm already employed, and I don't intend to leave my ministry for a government appointment."

The lady kept her polite voice and answered, "Nothing to worry about. All the commissioners will keep their jobs because we are looking for people from different sectors of our national life but people of integrity and people who have already shown their heart for the healing and reconciliation of our people."

Then with excitement, joy, and strong conviction, I answered, "On those terms, count me in."

The mission of the National Unity and Reconciliation Commission was to look into our past and identify the deep roots of the ethnic divisions that have characterized our nation over four decades, to put in place a policy that would guide the national journey towards healing and reconciliation, and to systematically monitor all the institutions in the country in order to prevent the re-sowing of the evil seeds of hatred.

On the first day of our induction, I silently lifted a short prayer before our meeting: "Lord, make us an instrument of healing and reconciliation in this nation and help me to play a significant role in this commission."

That first meeting was interestingly confusing. Once through with the introductions, nobody seemed to know exactly where to start this business. We had a few politicians from different sectors except from the Judicial, we had a Roman Catholic priest, myself from the Protestant churches, someone from the Muslim faith, and a few other people from the civil sector (non-government organizations and the media). Those from the political arena came with their constant attempt to play it straight and remain politically correct and in line with the political agenda. Others came with the conviction that this was a mission that called for innovation, ready to explore the different corners of the country and the world for solutions. You can imagine that with this kind of team the debates were intense but directionless.

A few months after our appointment, the country went through political turmoil that ended up with the resignation of the Speaker of the Parliament, followed by a resignation of the Prime Minister and the whole Cabinet, and finally the resignation of the President. This was a scary time, but it turned out to be a hidden blessing for the nation. The Vice-President at the time, General Paul Kagame, became President. A few weeks after he was sworn in, we met him to get his mind on our role in the new dispensation. We were waiting for guidelines and marching orders, but he reassured us and commissioned us again to find the solutions.

"We did not appoint you to rubber stamp anything from us. Go out, talk to the population, visit other countries, suggest solutions, and be assured that reconciliation is high on our Government agenda. This nation will not go far in its development without reconciliation, and we are ready to pay any price to see it happen."

I like this kind of confident speech, and deep inside I was shouting "YES!" I don't like playing it safe, and I'm not very good at political correctness. I love exploring issues, finding solutions, and making things happen, even when people will not applaud. I vividly recall my excitement when we left his office.

We first established an improvised action plan. Initially, we would engage in mass grassroots consultations, talking to different spheres of the community and finding where people thought the country had gone wrong in its past policies, politics, and practices. Then we would listen to their fears and concerns and find what they would like to see happen in the future. Finally, we would organize a national summit to present our findings before drafting a national policy for reconciliation. The policy would include the tenets and principles of our National Unity and Reconciliation and convert them into curricula for population education with clear Early Warning Systems (EWAS) and a tool we called the national reconciliation barometer. It was fascinating to work in this context. I love preaching, I love talking to people, but I also love strategizing, devising paths for transformation, and seeing them implemented.

We visited different countries that have suffered from divisions and have come out of them. We visited Germany and invited different dignitaries from Germany to visit us to share their experience of how they had handled the post-Holocaust situation after 1945. From their experience, we picked up some valuable principles. We visited South Africa to learn from their Truth and Reconciliation Commission, and some of their people came to train our commission. Finally, we went to Northern Ireland to hear how they had tried to reconcile their English and Irish factions. Eventually, we came together again to create a recipe from our international shopping. Some of the trips proved very fruitful, while others were largely polite exchanges but barren of applicable lessons. From the Germans we learned how to segregate the offenders into different categories in order to facilitate justice. We learned the important lesson of punishing the criminals but adding an element of clemency for the ordinary people who had been misled by the political leadership. We learned principles of social rehabilitation for those who took part in the killings. And we learned the importance of putting strong laws in place that are explicitly restrictive of political tendencies that might lead the nation back to divisive and genocidal ideologies. From South Africa we picked up the importance of speaking the truth but with the conscious intent to forgive those who would confess their crimes. I have to confess that not much was gleaned from Northern Ireland! Their differences have a complexity of their own and have grown deep roots into their politics that it will take time to uproot.

One significant lesson I learnt from the different trips was that a good number of countries have gone through troubles and ethnic/racial divisions, and when they came out, they celebrated peace without doing anything to heal the wounds of the past, to reshape the minds of the people, or to plan peace for the younger generations to come. During that period, I remember attending a conference in Ottawa for people who have suffered from genocides and ethnic or racial oppression. There were representatives from the Jewish communities, from the first nations in Canada, the American Indians from the USA, the Maori from New Zealand, the aboriginals of Australia, Armenians from Turkey, people from Cambodia, and some from South American countries. The different presentations done at the conference confirmed my assumption that many groups and countries have gone through genocide and mass killings but not many have done much to help their people heal from the wounds of their past. These unhealed wounds remain like sores on the collective mind, and you feel the groaning and anger in the voice of generations that have not even known the suffering. While physical wounds are never transmitted from father to son, wounds of the heart become engrained in the genetics of a group or nation if they are not well treated. The consequences are heavy in terms of a broken spirit or a revengeful mindset that triggers on-going fears and retaliation tendencies in the nations.

By the time my turn came to speak, which was towards the end of the conference, I apologized to the organizers and audience and told them I had slightly changed the content of my presentation. While I would share about the suffering of the Tutsis in Rwanda, I would share a bit more on my personal healing from the wounds of my past, linking that healing to how Rwanda was finding healing and reconciliation in our nation. I spoke with passion about the importance of focusing on healing the minds of our people. I explained to these many groups that it is counterproductive to keep your mind in a recrimination and reclamation mode that keeps you in a state of mental victimhood and anger because that distorts your vision of life and your outlook of people.

By the time I finished my presentation, what was a conference had turned into ministry. The whole hall stood up in loud ovation, and you could see tears flowing on many faces. I collected hugs and trophies! I still have the regalia I received from a Mohawk chief who came to me and confessed that the talk had helped him to understand why the youth in his community were finding it difficult to integrate into the mainstream of life in Canada. "We have been given more than we need to propel ourselves higher than most in the nation, but we are stuck on the ground. When you spoke about spirits that react like broken springs that cannot bounce back, about people who prefer to stay in wounded victimhood that leads them into inactivity and despondency, I could easily feel and identify with that. I could see all the younger generation in my community who are killing themselves with drugs instead of using the resources we have to push ahead in life." He took his beads off and put them around my neck, he wrapped his chief's red sache around my waist, and embraced me through his tears.

An old Jewish lady gave me a golden necklace with the star of David and told me, "Give this to one of those young survivors of the genocide in your home. Tell her this is a gift from an old grandmother who has suffered from the holocaust when I was a child. Tell her to listen to your wisdom. Today, you have helped me understand why I have lived all these years trapped in the memories of my past wounds and using them to justify my despondency. I have gone from conference to conference just to listen to people bemoaning what we have suffered, suggesting reactive behaviors that kept fueling my anger, condemning the world that came too late to our rescue, not knowing that it does not contribute to any positive change. Tell the young people that it does not pay and ask them not to take that path into the future. Preach that message again and again and help them as you helped me today."

I have experienced the same response in different conferences around the world, which tells me the world needs to hear the message of healing, confession, and reconciliation that we have learned to preach. People understand it better when it is made personal, when they can identify their problems in what you present, and when they can see the benefit of paying the price of repentance and forgiveness. Reconciliation is a tough decision to make. It is sacrificial, but it is a fountain of reward for the rest of your life.

I served four terms (12 years) on that prestigious commission, and for three terms I was the Vice-Chairperson. My joy was never in the frequent rubbing of shoulders with the influential people in Government and the diplomatic corps; it was in knowing that we were shaping a better nation for ourselves and for our children after us. I was on the Commission's task force that distilled the national policy for reconciliation, and it was thrilling to see the policy slowly taking shape from the piles of papers that had been collected from countless seminars and workshops, grassroots consultations, government conversations, and national summits. Our task force worked for months, trying to find a framework we could use to unify all the elements we had collected.

We finally came to an "aha moment" when one evening I was silently praying for a way forward while listening to a program on the radio where children were playing with Kinyarwanda riddles. One of the kids gave this riddle: "*Nyoko na mama bapfaga iki?*" (What was the cause of the conflict between your mother and my mother?) And the answer was "*Akayuzi ko mu rubibi*" (That little pumpkin plant that sprouted between our two gardens"). This little riddle ignited an inspiration in my mind! Conflict is always the consequence of an unmet, felt need! The insight spiraled me into Maslow's Hierarchy of Human Needs: physical, safety, belonging, esteem, and self-actualization needs. I went back to the pile of notes I had on my table and spent the evening playing with a classification of all the reasons people had given that had led to the genocide against the Tutsis, but also to the solutions they had suggested to escape from its fallout. Everything slotted neatly into the framework. Beginning the next day, the discussions flowed so easily that the draft of the policy was finished in a few days.

From the policy, we developed curricula and programs to educate the population and the younger generation for peace and reconciliation. In the process we added other documents like the Early Warning Systems, which would allow us to detect any shift in locus of conflict in our national life. We developed the Reconciliation Barometer, which helps to evaluate the progress of healing in the nation, and we suggested strict laws that will prevent people from sowing seeds of ethnic divisions again. If you ever hear people saying that Rwanda has very restrictive laws on speech, believe it. It is forbidden and punishable by law to negate the genocide against the Tutsis or belittle it. It is forbidden to use an ethnic justification for any political agenda. It is forbidden to segregate or discriminate against any Rwandan citizen based on ethnic origins. Very tough laws.

A group of students from an American university once asked me a provocative question, pointing out how intolerant we are on what they called "freedom of speech." I answered with another question: "What do doctors do when you have a broken leg? Do they allow you to go out and play soccer?"

The students said, "No, the doctors put the broken leg into a solid cast until the bones have knitted well back together."

Then I told them: "That's exactly what we have done. We have put in place very restrictive laws so that our broken nation can heal, and when we are sure it is well healed, we will revisit and revise those laws."

They were impatient to know when, and my final answer was, "It does not matter how long it will take. What matters is that we see our country well healed." As Americans are increasingly realizing, the failure to heal wounds truly will always show itself in time. The poorly healed fracture will break again.

I hope and keep praying that by the time I die, I will be able to look back and say, "At least I have given my contribution to the building of a better nation." I have enjoyed the exercise so much that I'm now working at taking reconciliation beyond the ethnic animosities and making it my daily lifestyle.

Chapter Ten

RECONCILIATION
AS A LIFESTYLE

"If it is possible, as far as it depends on you, live at peace with everyone"
Romans 12:18

WRITING A BOOK has been compared to giving birth to a child! It starts with conception and pregnancy, then comes labor and delivery. I do not know what kind of child I would call this book when I consider the span of more than twenty years between its conception and its final delivery. And that is not where the comparison is leading anyway. The birth of a child is probably the most transformative experience in a couple's life. It is the beginning of a new chapter without an end in view. Likewise, the writing of this book has introduced a new chapter in my life. It has spurred me into the quest for a new philosophy of life, a new approach to daily relationships. I want reconciliation to be my lifestyle.

I do not want to be just another preacher of reconciliation; beyond that, I want to be both a reconciled person and a reconciler. An American student once asked me: "Why did you choose to engage in this work of reconciliation? What motivated you? What does it mean for your life?"

I paused for a while and then answered, "Well, when you are born in a broken country, a broken family, as a matter of fact a broken world, at one point you have to make a choice either to become bitter, cynical, and destructive, or to forgive and make reconciliation your lifestyle. I lived for years following the first option, and I know its consequences well. Eventually, when I came to the Lord, I was introduced to a different perspective on people and circumstances, and I have intentionally chosen to make reconciliation my lifestyle and my life mission. I want to age like an African banana, going from green and sour to yellow, ripe, and sweet, whereas many people go like banana juice that starts sweet and moves to become a bitter cider." The answer sounded inspirational and received enthusiastic applause. But one smart student asked me to elaborate on the topic, and after a few sentences I promised they would read it in a book I was writing! That is how this reflection was born!

The word reconciliation is often reduced to its political content, to the peaceful coexistence of former antagonists, and its simple mention usually brings to mind only racial or ethnic relationships. So the first step in the journey towards a reconciled life is to depoliticize the term and make it personal. True reconciliation starts within the individual. It is an inner reality lived in the heart before it is expressed outside in words, attitudes, and deeds. Unless reconciliation and peace start with the individual heart, it will remain in the realm of lofty rhetoric without touching reality. I have attended conferences on reconciliation where half of the talks were all full of acrid recriminations that sounded like hate speech. I have met preachers of reconciliation who were as bitter as a green lemon. I have sat with people who spoke of peace while fuming with anger and hatred or crumbling under a heavy burden of guilt and shame. Such a universe of "un-grace," to use Philip Yancey's term, leaves no breathing space for peace and reconciliation. Our world is full of competition, jealousies, selfish ambition, and all types of folly of grandeur. We are daily bombarded with publicity that feeds our fears and fuels our greed and ambitions. We rush, we push, we step on each other's toes, and we impose our views. The human race is perpetually caught up in a disgraceful rat race that we have accepted as normal life. The Romans had a proverb, "si vis pacem, para bellum" (if you want peace, prepare for war). It is as if the world has borrowed the words and turned them into a life motto. And the Bible concludes, "The way of peace they do not know; there is no justice in their paths. They have turned them into crooked roads; no one who walks in them will know peace" (Is. 59:8). Every individual, even when alone, is a walking interior war, and we cannot give peace to others when we do not have it in ourselves. The path to peace must pass through our inner life, which is why the Bible says, "above all else guard your heart, for it is the wellspring of life" (Prov. 4:23).

In the children's cartoon *Avatar: The Last Airbender*, Guru Pathik gives Aang a list of emotions that block people from being positive influences in life. He mentions fear, guilt, shame, grief, self-rejection, self-deception, and ambition. These are inner hindrances that choke life. Jesus himself insisted on this reality when he said, "Out of a man's heart comes evil thoughts, sexual immorality, theft, murder, adultery, greed, malice, deceit, lewdness, envy, slander, arrogance and folly. All these evils come from inside and make a man 'unclean'" (Mark 7:21-23). This is a crucial list of emotions to keep in check all day long; these are unwanted, destructive guests that keep knocking on the door of our hearts but should never be allowed in. A close analysis of the hate speeches that fueled the genocide against the Tutsis in Rwanda shows that fear and selfish ambition were the main fuel of hatred. We always hate and will even kill what we fear!

The emotional fallout of the genocide came in the form of grief, anger, and bitterness on the side of the survivors, and shame and guilt on the side of the perpetrators. These disastrous emotions put us again in the spiral of fear and hatred, a hidden landmine that if undetonated will explode into future violence! The road to real peace will consist of living a life pruned of fear, anger, grief, shame, guilt, and self- condemnation. This is where the message of the cross of Jesus Christ becomes central to the message of reconciliation.

The first two chapters of the Bible give us a clear picture of genuine reconciliation. In the beginning was peace, in the beginning was harmony. Adam and Eve lived in peace and harmony with God, with themselves, with each other, and with creation. God was the Creator, the King and the Provider; Man was the overseer. This symbiotic coexistence was destroyed by sin. Adam and Eve lost their peace as guilt introduced them to shame and fear of their own nakedness. The consequent emotional spiral brought alienation from God, as they went hiding under the bushes, and to alienation from each other and from nature, as they chose to blame each other instead of owning their disobedience. Adam and Eve refused the route of recognition of sin, repentance, and confession, which would have attracted God's forgiveness. God killed an animal, covered their nakedness, and activated his alternate plan for salvation. God is still on mission, pursuing reconciliation with people who keep running away from him. Hence, reconciliation with self, with each other, and with nature remains elusive! We are born facing the wrong direction, and we keep running away from our shadows that are projected ahead of us by the light of God shining behind us. It is only when we turn around and walk in the light that we are in real communion, and the blood of Jesus washes us of all our sins (1 John 1:7).

God's answer to the need for reconciliation came through the cross of Jesus Christ. The cross speaks with final certainty of the love of God for us, and only people who have understood how much they are loved will dare love as he loved us. The cross speaks of pardon and forgiveness. Those who understand they are forgiven will never be afraid to repent and confess. On the cross, Jesus took our pains, our sorrows, and our infirmities upon himself, and he calls us to imitate him — he calls us to heal and forgive. Jesus carried our sins and our iniquities and made peace with God. At the foot of the cross the offender finds solace, hearing Jesus pray to the Father to forgive his offenders, and it is at the foot of the cross that the offended can put down their woundedness and forgive. By his cross, Jesus killed the enmity that was between us and reconciled us with God, paving the road for reconciliation with each other. It is at the foot of the cross that we find level ground, where the offender and the offended find common ground for reconciliation. Reconciliation is the heart of the Gospel and is the only hope for humanity. It is only those who have been forgiven who can forgive. It is only those who know the grace of God who can confess their sins without fear of condemnation. And it is such people who will become ambassadors of reconciliation. When you have tasted the sweetness of a reconciled life, you cannot keep it to yourself! You cannot stop telling others about it.

When you contemplate Jesus Christ hanging on the cross, with his enemies jeering and insulting, and you hear him praying for them, you are challenged to a different lifestyle, a lifestyle of reconciliation and love for enemies. Paul puts it so well when he writes, "We who with unveiled faces contemplate the Lord's glory, are being transformed into his likeness with ever-increasing glory, which comes from the Lord, who is the Spirit" (2 Cor. 3:18). A new definition of reconciliation emerges and a new picture of a reconciled life is painted as we intentionally receive transformation into the likeness of Christ. A reconciled life is a life that is lived to reflect the character of Jesus Christ, and the character of Jesus is the fruit of the Spirit.

In his letter to the Galatians, Paul describes the universe of "un-grace" full of "sexual immorality, impurity and debauchery; idolatry and witchcraft; hatred, discord and jealousy, fits of rage, selfish ambition, dissensions, factions and envy, drunkenness, orgies and the like. . . . Those who live like this will not inherit the Kingdom of God" (Gal. 5:19–21). I would easily translate this conclusion and say, those who live like this will not build a world of reconciliation; those who live like this will never know peace and harmony with themselves, with their neighbors, with God. Paul hastens to give us a different way of life, a far better way. "But the fruit of the Spirit is love, peace, joy, patience, kindness, goodness, faithfulness, gentleness and self-control" (Gal. 5:22–23). This fruitfulness is the portrait of Christlikeness and is what is reflected from the cross of Jesus. Love, peace, and joy make the atmosphere of a reconciled life. This is a life of loving like Christ, certainly loving your friends, and loving those who are lovely and lovable, but also loving your enemies, the unloving, the unlovable, and even those who refuse to be loved. Loving where you are, loving what you do, loving everybody and everything around you is the secret of a reconciled, fulfilled life. I have found out that all the other fruit are a product of love! When you love what you do, you never feel stress even when the work lasts for hours. When you love where you live, you do not feel like emigrating elsewhere. When you love the people you work with, it is always a great joy to wake up in the morning and go to work. When you do everything out of love, your life and your service become agreeable to you and to others.

The journey of love, and its companions of peace and joy, is the most exciting journey in life. Every day, I wake up and tell myself, this is another day, this is another occasion to love. The fruit of the Spirit has become my daily morning prayer, and I find myself calling on the Spirit to pour more of it when I fall short. And I often fall short of the target, which is when the Lord reminds me, "There's nothing to worry about. My love for you is not based on your performance. It is all by grace." But I know, the more I try to live the fruit of the Spirit, the more I am gradually transformed to reflect the character of Christ. These words from 2 Corinthians 13:14, "the grace of our Lord Jesus-Christ, the love of God the Father and the fellowship of the Holy Spirit," have gained a new meaning in this challenging journey. I forgive myself, I forgive others, and I can afford to forgive because I know

I am loved despite my human limitations and shortcomings. I have been forgiven, I am loved, and I am empowered by God to accept my humanity with its limitations and flaws. Forgiven to forgive others and myself.

People love challenges. They climb mountains, they ride motorcycles, and drive sport cars at dizzying, neck-breaking speeds, looking for a thrill, looking for victory. But is there any challenge greater than love? Is there any conquest greater than conquering your own character? Is there any greater challenge than loving those who refuse to change, those who oppose, those who slander, those who betray, those who reject? Many people love and sing the victory of the resurrection, but behind it there is the greater victory of the cross! We are daily crucified on the cross of a universe of ungrace, but when we think about it, we are daily victorious when we show love where we encounter hatred, when we show patience with people in the traffic jam of the daily human rat race. What a life, what a mission! And only reconciled lives will be whole material to build such a world of peace and wholistic reconciliation.

Will you accept the grace to be such a man or woman, who will accept maturation into a sweet banana rather than turn into an acrid cider? Will you live by the law of love, peace, joy, kindness, patience, meekness, and gentleness rather than go by the law of the "superman," who like the character of Lamech in the book of Genesis promised to revenge seven times for one offense? Will you strive to sow the seeds of peace and leave every place, every life, far better than it was before you arrived? Will you make reconciliation your philosophy of life, your lifestyle? That's the challenge I have given myself in every detail of daily life, and I leave it with you to ponder and decide to live *Reconciliation as a Lifestyle*.

GLOSSARY

Afandi: Military officer, roughly equivalent to "superior."

Batwa, or Twa: The smallest minority ethnic group in Rwanda, accounting for about 1% of the population. They are a pygmy people who lived traditionally in forest areas as hunter-gatherers. They occupy a socially inferior position in Rwandan society.

Biheko: Traditional East African deity worshipped in parts of Rwanda, Uganda, Burundi, and Congo, and associated especially with fertility.

Equilibre Ethnique: Literally, "ethnic balance," the ethnically based quota system developed after independence. It became a political tool to limit the number of Tutsis in government, universities, utilities, and other positions of influence.

Gikari: The open, rear area of an enclosed compound behind the house. The area for domestic tasks, including cooking, winnowing grain, slaughtering animals, and cleaning dishes.

Hutu: The largest of the three major ethnic groups who settled in Rwanda, comprising just over 80% of the population. Distinct for an agricultural way of life, they were oppressed by the Belgian colonial administration in favor of the Tutsi.

Interahamwe: Literally, "Those who attack together." Local militias of extremist Hutus organized for the persecution and eventual extermination of the Tutsi minority.

Inyenzi: Cockroaches. The favorite term of abuse applied to Tutsis in genocidal propaganda.

Kinyarwanda: The language of Rwandans, including all its ethnic groups.

Kwihutura: Literally, "to take off your Hutu belonging." Figuratively, to move into the cattle-keeping, ruling class.

Kwita Izina: The traditional naming ceremony in Rwandan culture, which includes all the children in a village offering names to the baby's aunts. Occurs about a month after a child's birth.

Machete: A short-handled agricultural tool with a long, broad blade primarily used for cutting branches and stalks. They were used as swords during the Genocide.

Murokore: A born-again Christian, usually associated with believers touched by the East African Revival. Someone who is clearly not a nominal Christian.

Mwami: The title of the King of Rwanda prior to Belgian occupation.

Mzungu: White person. Also figuratively used of Rwandans who display their wealth in ostentatious ways.

Qur'an: Arabic language collection of Allah's revelations to Muhammad given in several instances over a period of years. The eventual Qur'an was chosen from among many different collections; all others were destroyed. Believed to exactly match a book in Allah's heaven.

RPF: Rwandan Patriotic Front. A Tutsi army organized within the Ugandan military and led by General Paul Kigame, Rwanda's current President. Its successful invasion in 1994 ended the 100-day genocide of the Tutsis.

Tutsi: One of the two ethnic minorities who settled Rwanda and anciently united the various tribes into a single Rwandan kingdom. Favored by the Belgian colonial administration, they became the object of Hutu animosity after Rwandan Independence in 1962. A genocide of the Tutsi was attempted in 1994, lasting 100 days and resulting in the death of at least 800,000 Tutsis.

Ubupfura: The honorable character associated with nobility and good leadership.

Glossary

✠ GAFCON
GLOBAL ANGLICAN FUTURE CONFERENCE

This book is an indirect result of the Global Anglican Future Conference, which is a movement of renewal within the global Anglican Church of Anglican Christians committed to holding fast to the Bible as the measure of the true Christian faith, and to proclaiming the unchanging, transforming Gospel of Jesus Christ. Responding to a long and steady compromise in morality and doctrine within parts of the Anglican Communion, particularly over issues of biblical authority, over a thousand clergy and lay leaders (representing the majority of the world's Anglicans) gathered in Jerusalem in 2008 and issued the Jerusalem Statement and Declaration, also establishing a permanent leadership council of Archbishops.

Through the GAFCON movement, a united Gospel mission of Anglicans around the world has reaffirmed the received faith of the Church. The powerful witness of Global South churches, often in the face of Islamic terrorism and militant nationalism, has given renewed vigor to Western Anglicans facing more subtle battles with cultural politics and moral decline. Evidence of this influence is apparent in the initial recognition at GAFCON 2008 of the Anglican Church in North America (ACNA) as a member Province of the Anglican Church. Through GAFCON, American Anglicans have direct, intentional relationship with sister churches in the Global South, such as the Anglican Church of Rwanda. The relationship of this book's authors developed through these links between GAFCON churches.

To learn more about GAFCON and the united mission of the Global Anglican Future Conference, go to *www.gafcon.org*. For more information about the mission in America, visit *www.anglicanchurch.net*.

In the precolonial kingdom of Rwanda, the walls of kings' and chiefs' residences were decorated with spiral and geometric designs painted with black, white, and red pigments. Thought to have been invented by Prince Kakira, the son of the king of Gisaka (now known as Kibungo, or the Eastern Province), **imigongo designs** are produced by mixing cow dung with ash, then molding raised geometric patterns that are dried in the sun. Colored paints created by organic material such as plants and clay are then applied to the dry panel. Prior to the 1994 Genocide, the craft was practiced throughout the country, but it was nearly lost due to the conflict. This art was resurrected in 2000 by a local women's cooperative in the village of Nyakarimbi, in the Eastern Province near the border of Tanzania. Named for the art's inventor, the Kakira Imigongo Cooperative now trains a new generation in this traditional art form.